TABLE OF CONTENTS

In appreciation of the countless color lovers
who gently participated in the crazy world of coloring and calming activity.

- Mayank Patel

Author has precisely selected sea creatures and created 51 Illustrations
to provoke your color sense to calm the mind.

In the Coloring Book, you'll enjoy 51 exclusive hand drawn artworks,
from fish designs to sea flora, from Mandalas to Pentangles, dolphin to octopus
and beautiful ocean creatures.

You'll surely provoke your imagination and color senses.
Spread out your imagination, color senses and
creative mind to occupy in the pleasurable calming activity.

Relax the nerve and unwind stress within the body.

Each Page is designed for fun and Relaxations,
Choice of coloring kits can be utilized
(color pens, color pencils, markers, crayons).

Adults and older kids who enjoy color can use
this special and exclusive coloring book
based on the LIFE OF OCEAN.

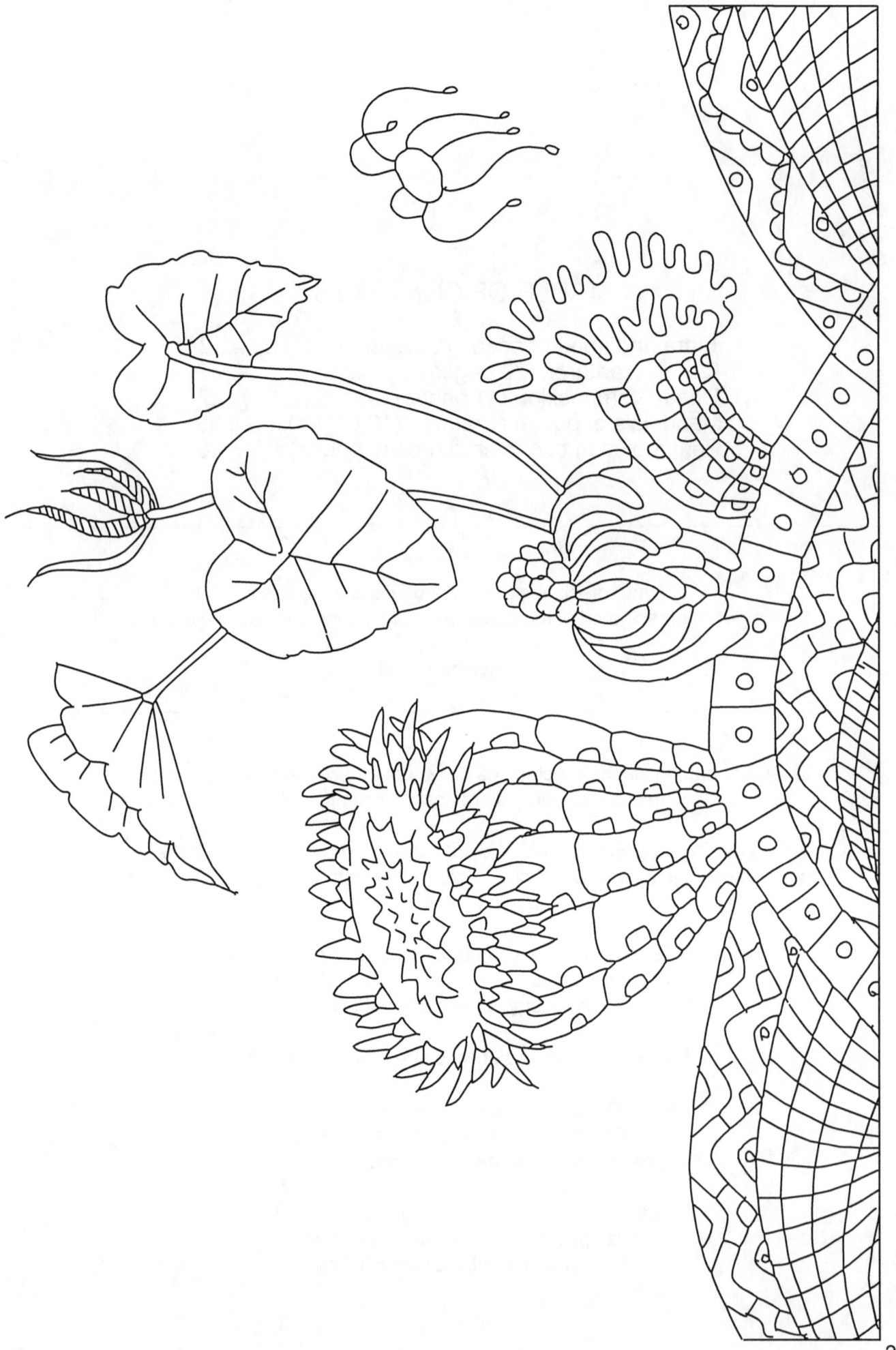

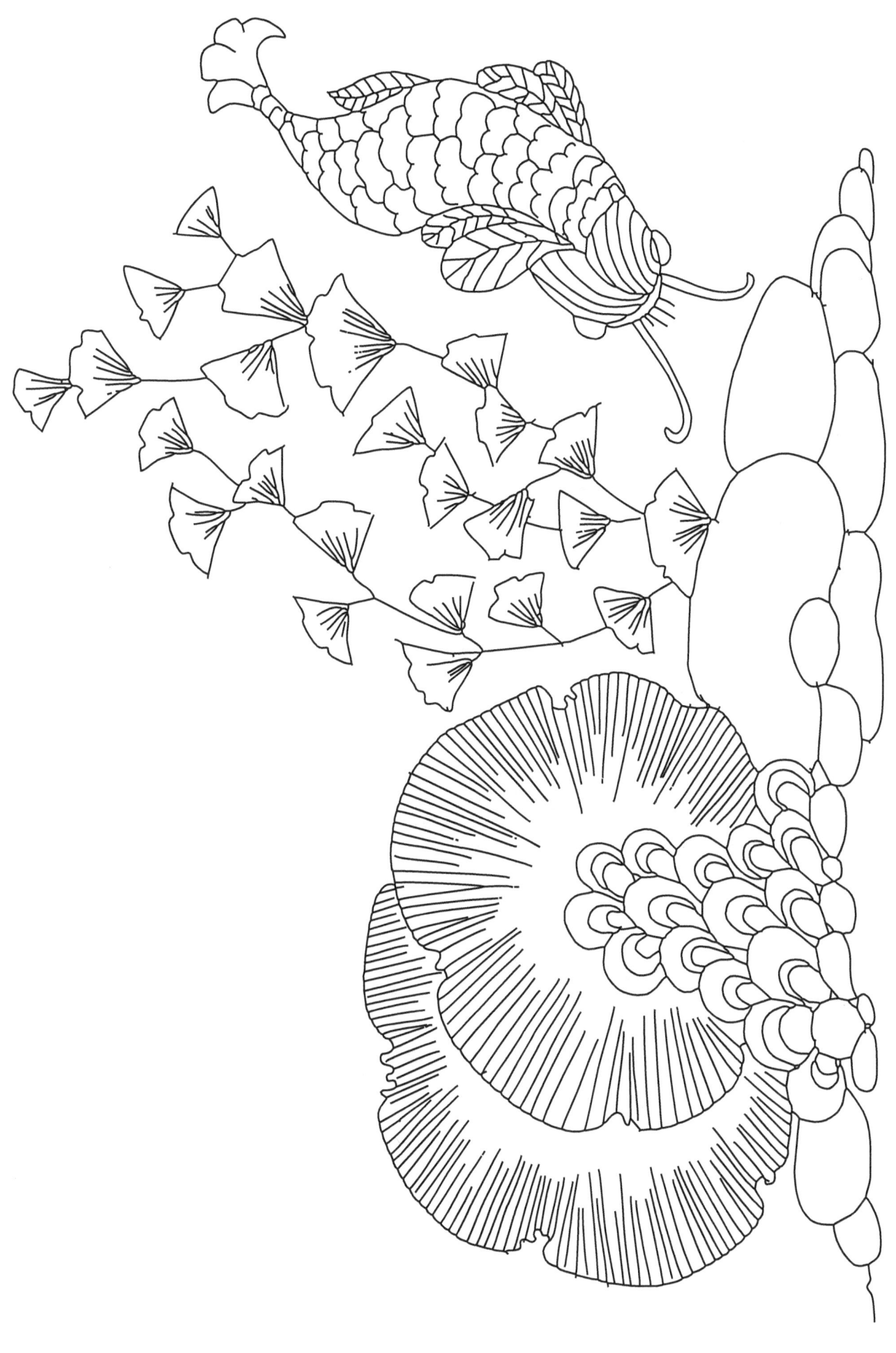

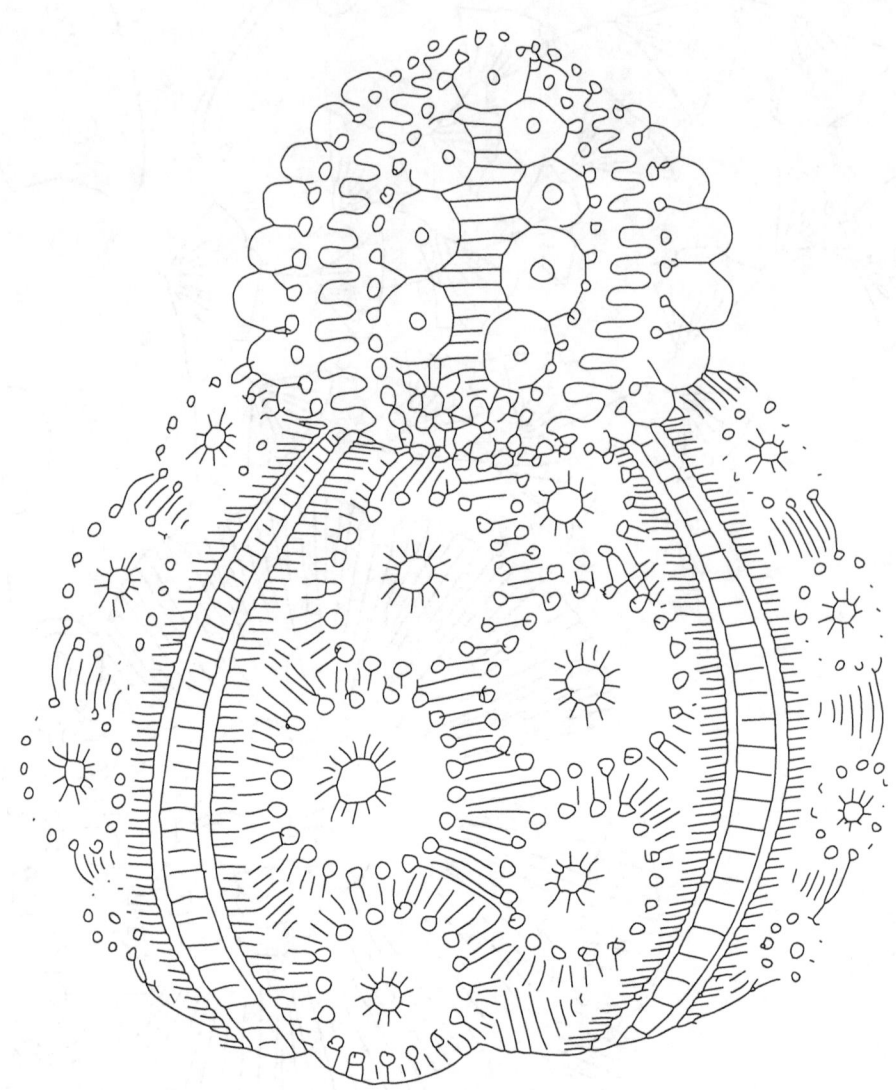

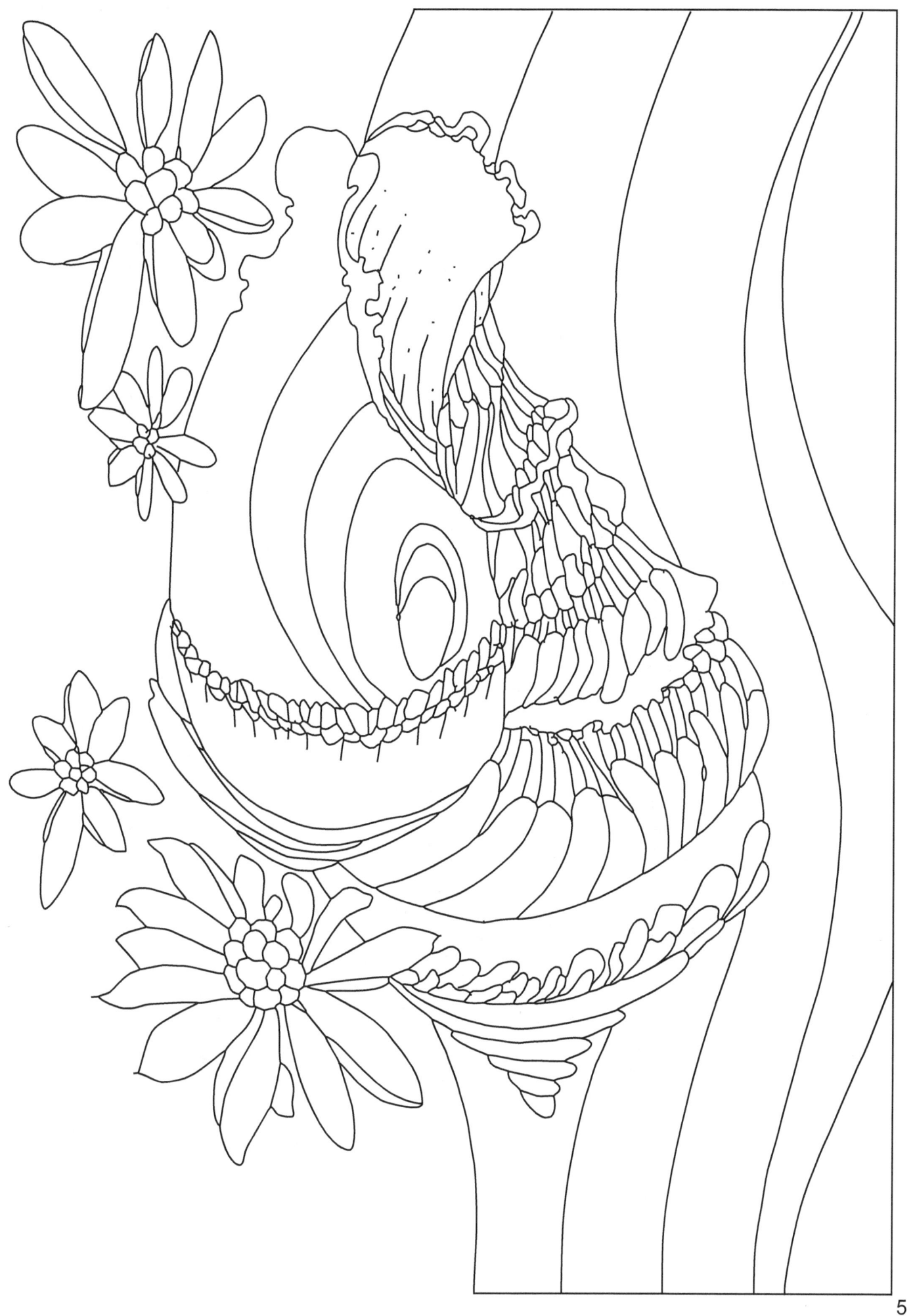

5

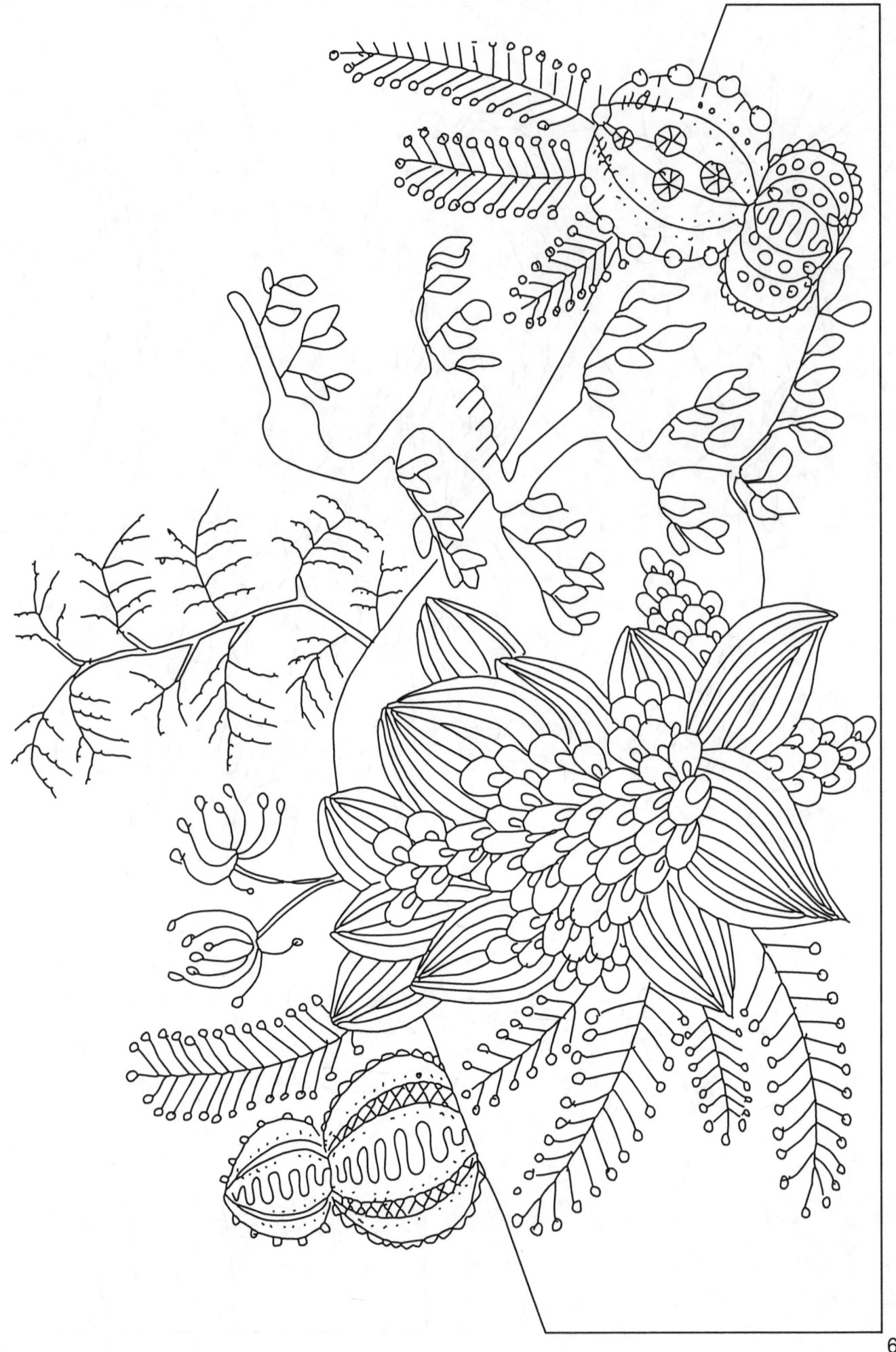

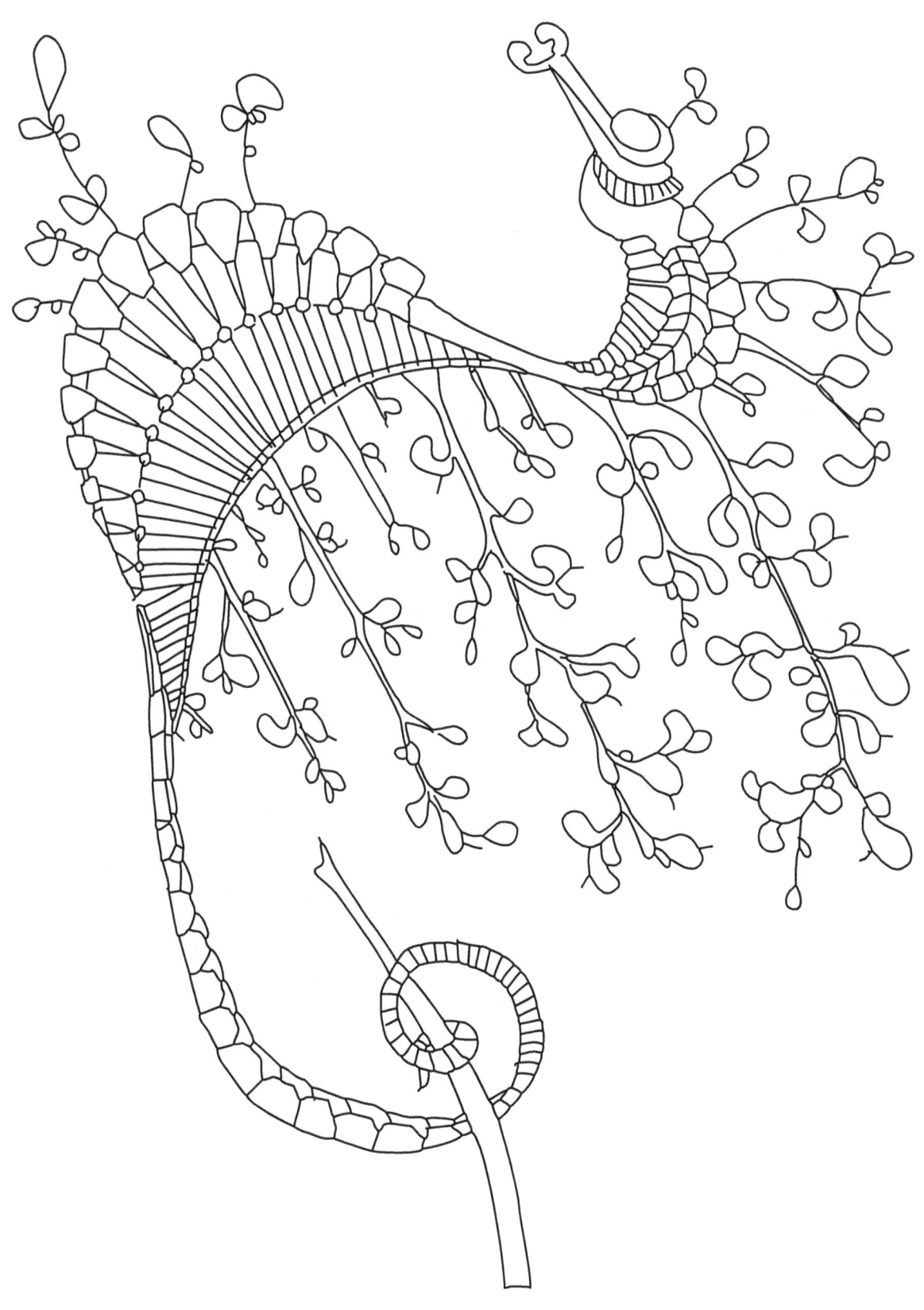

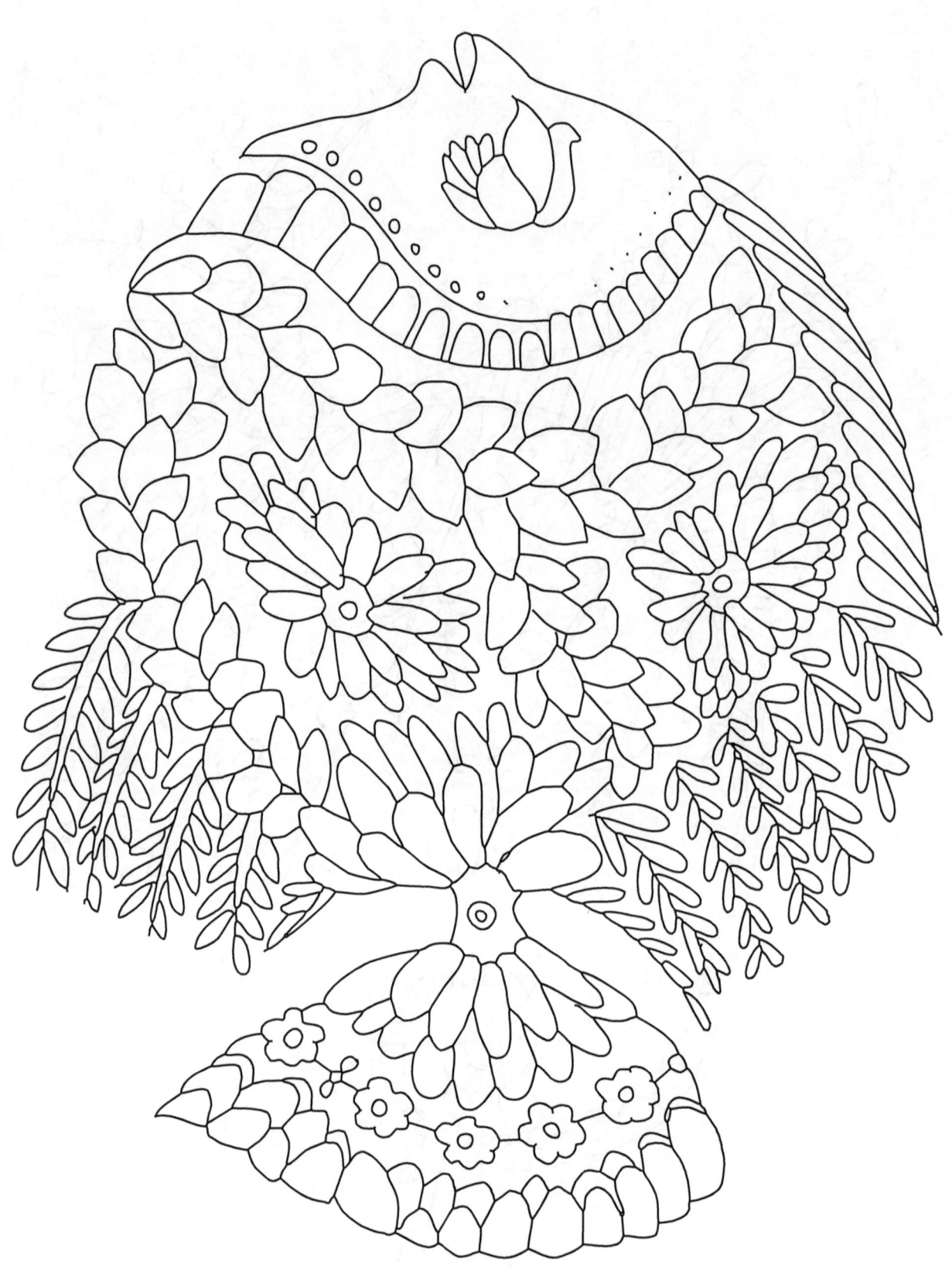

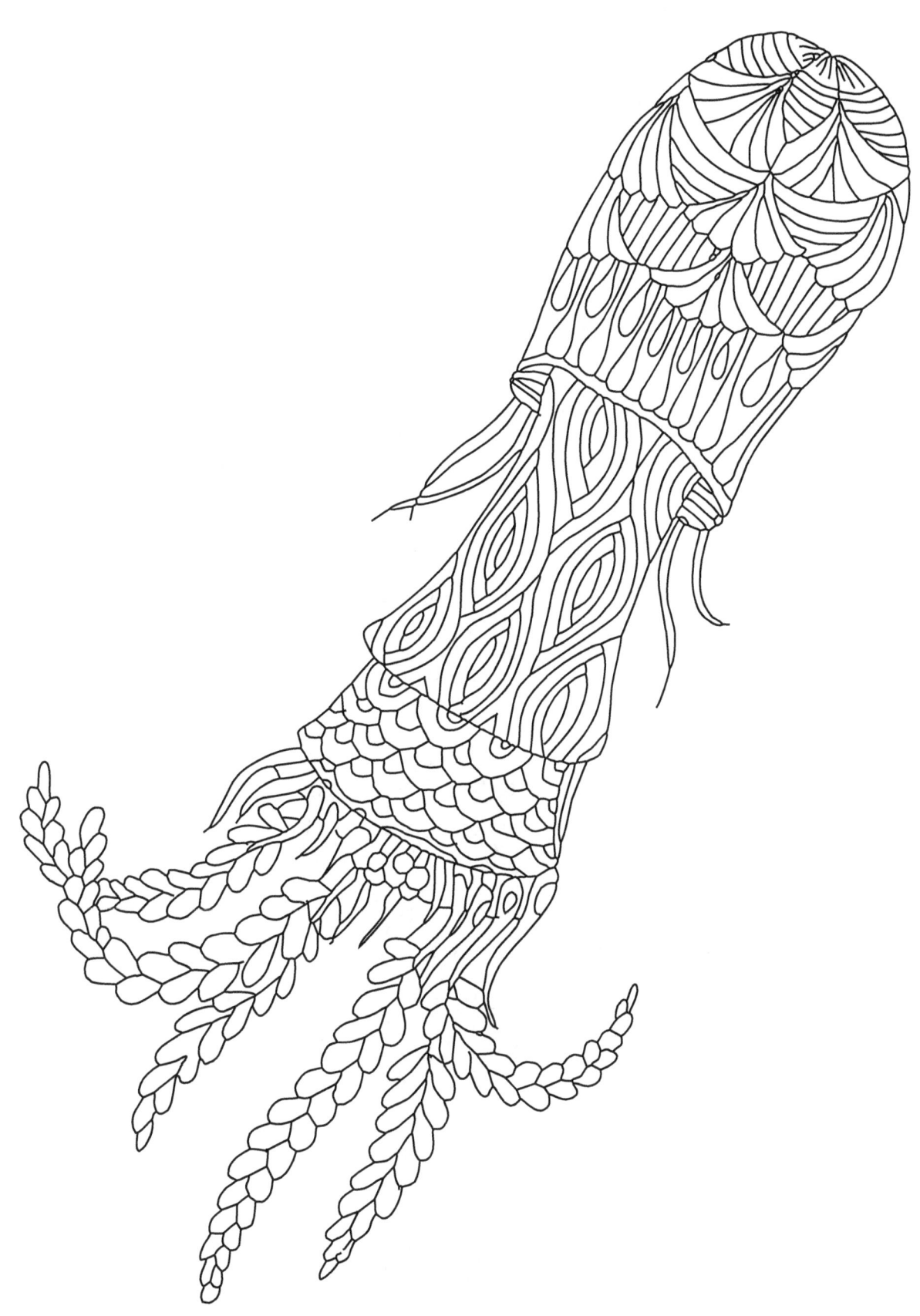

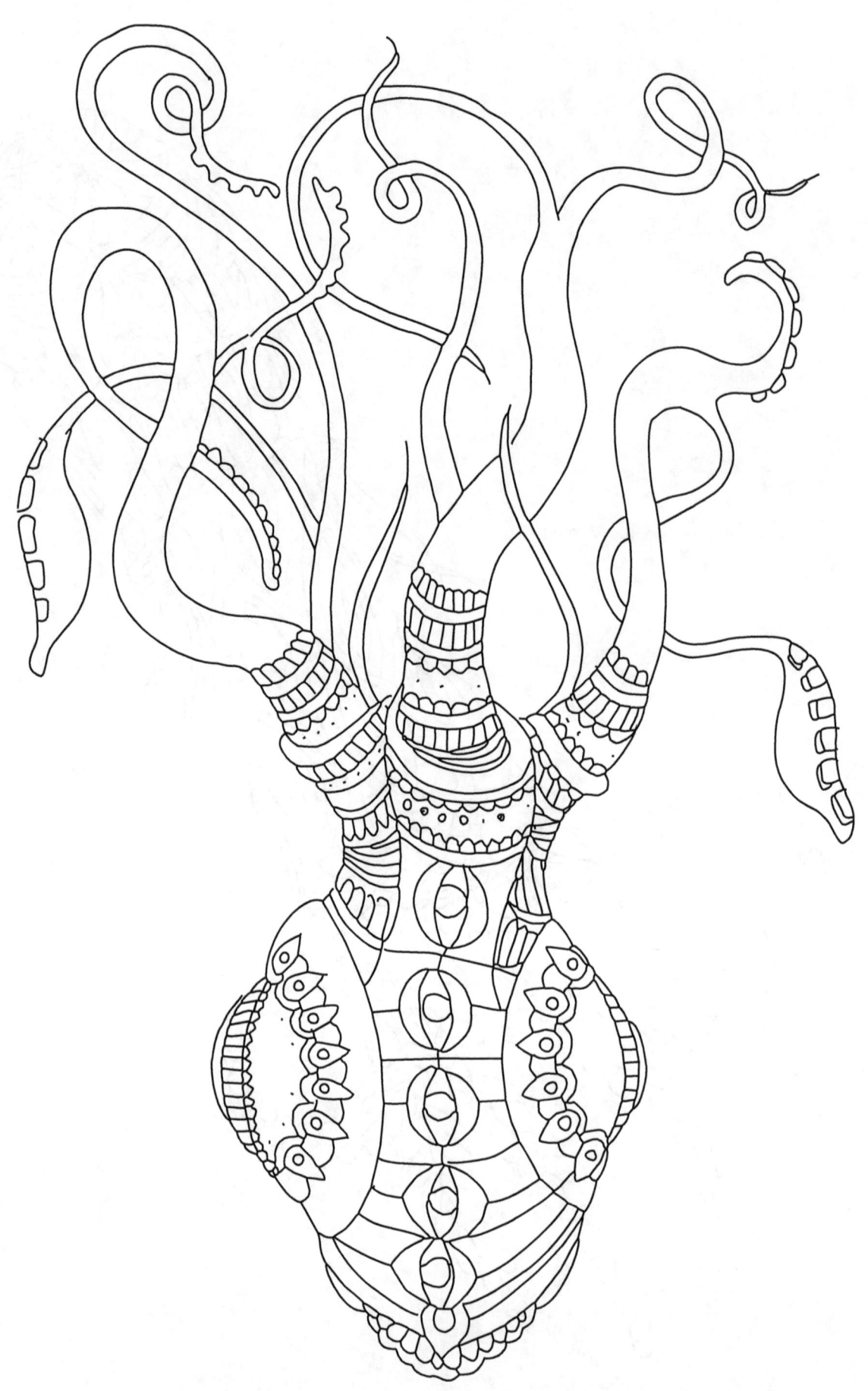

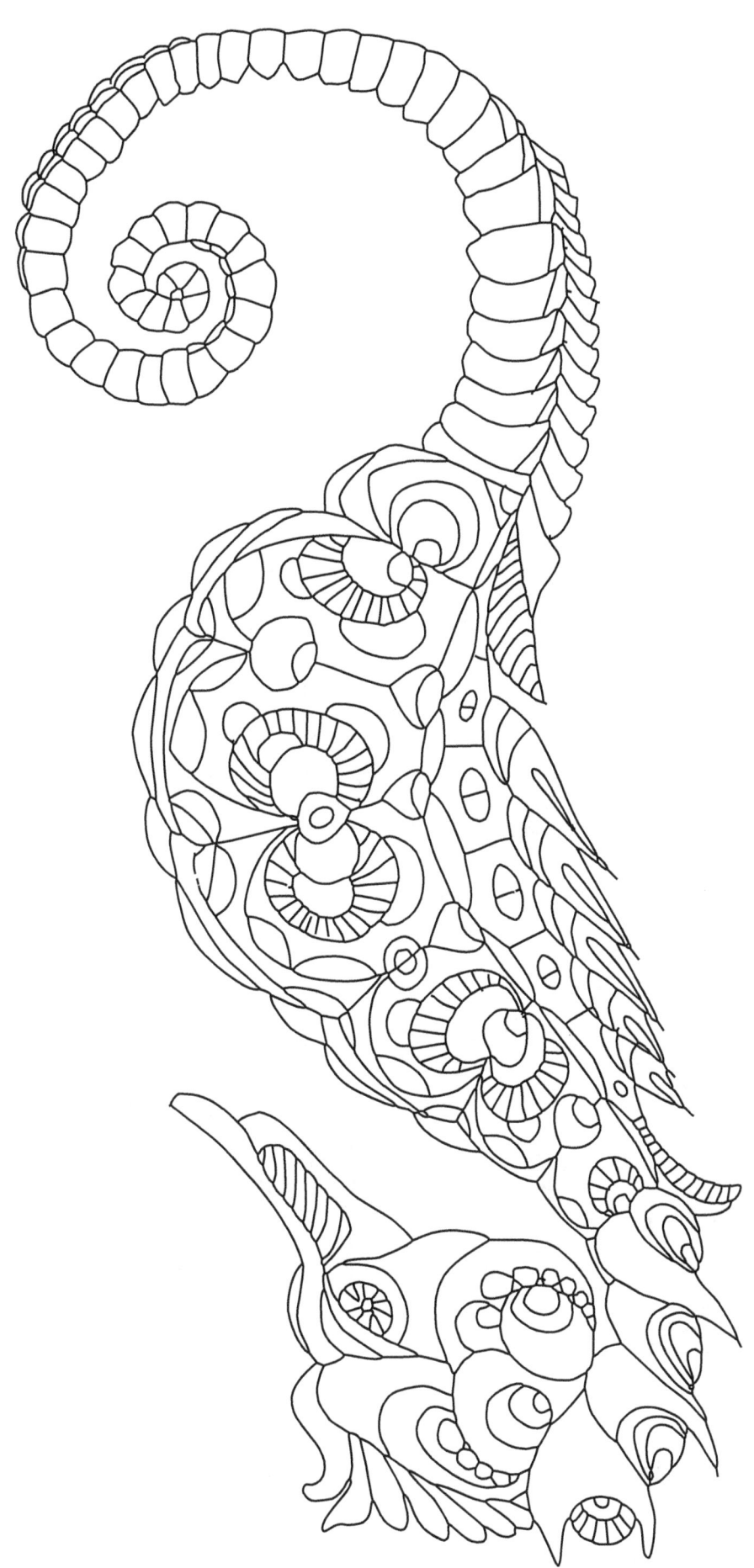

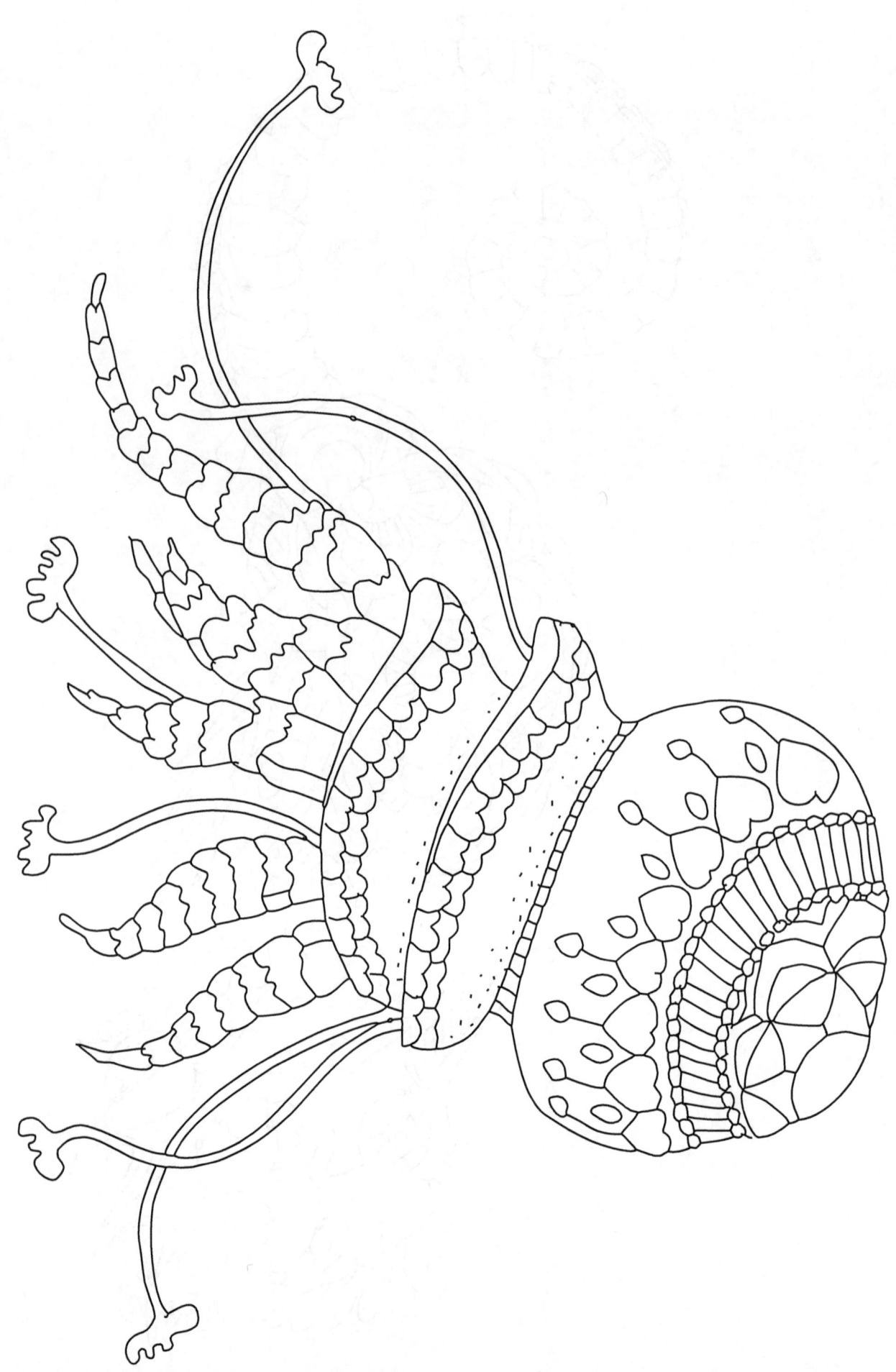

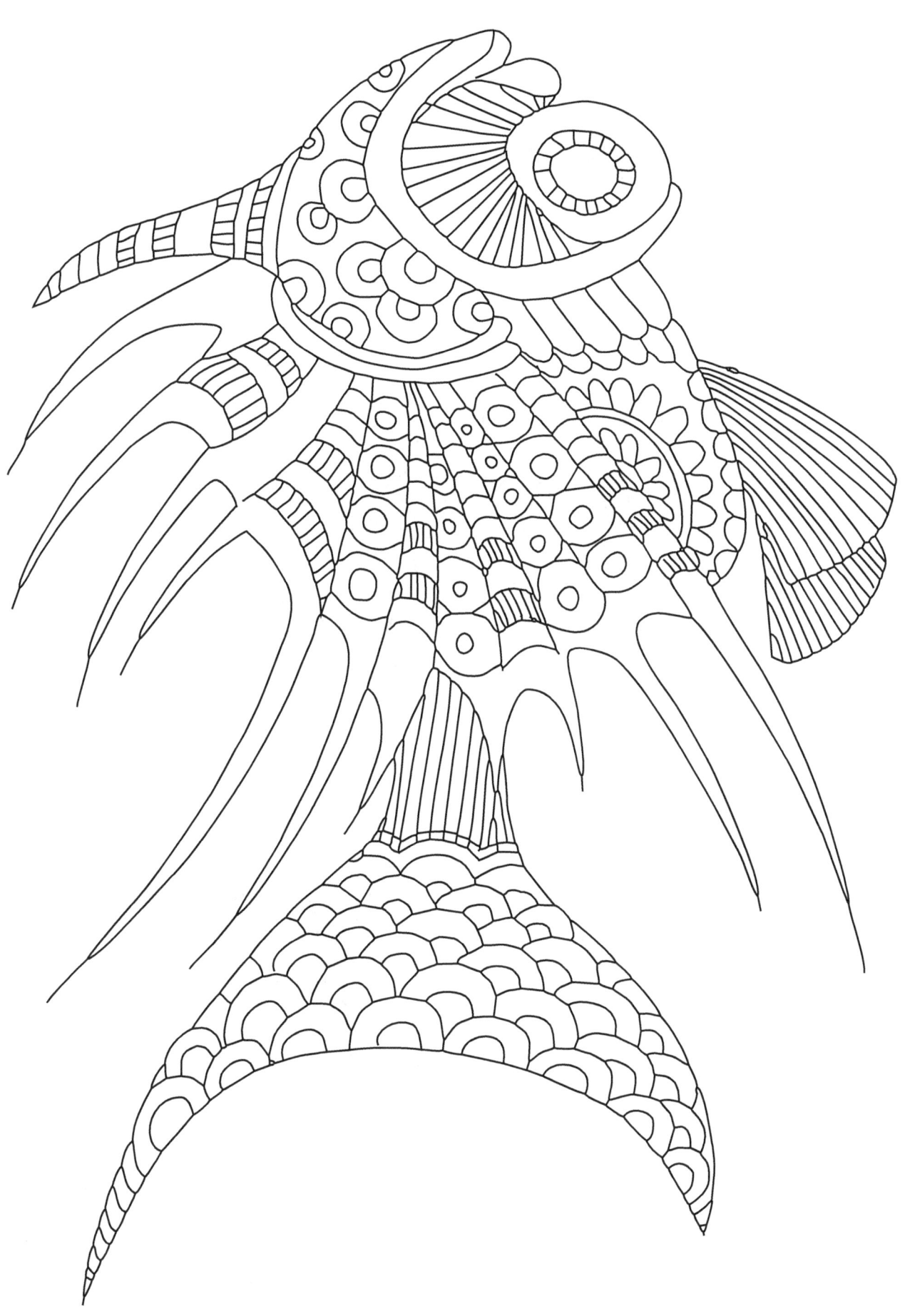

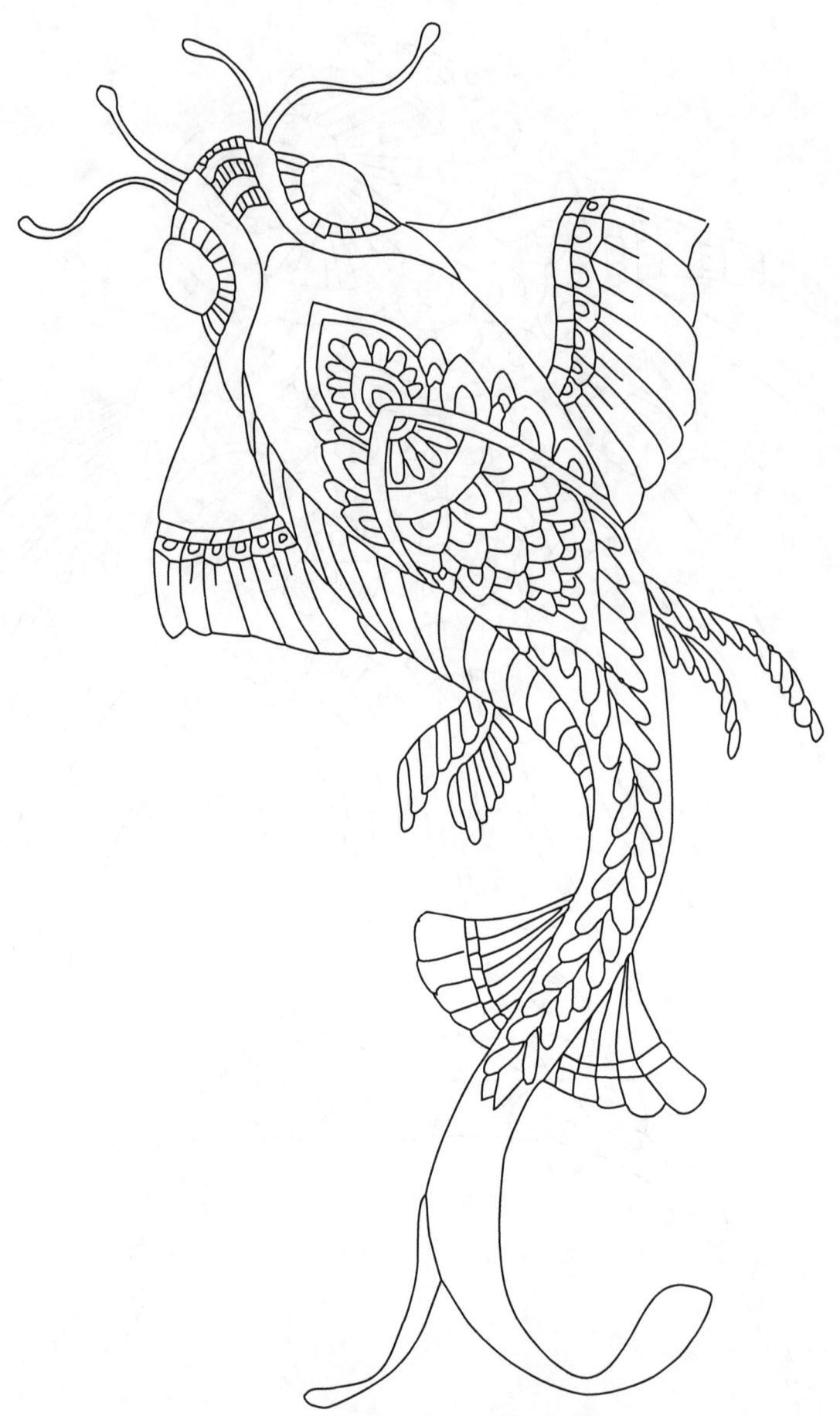

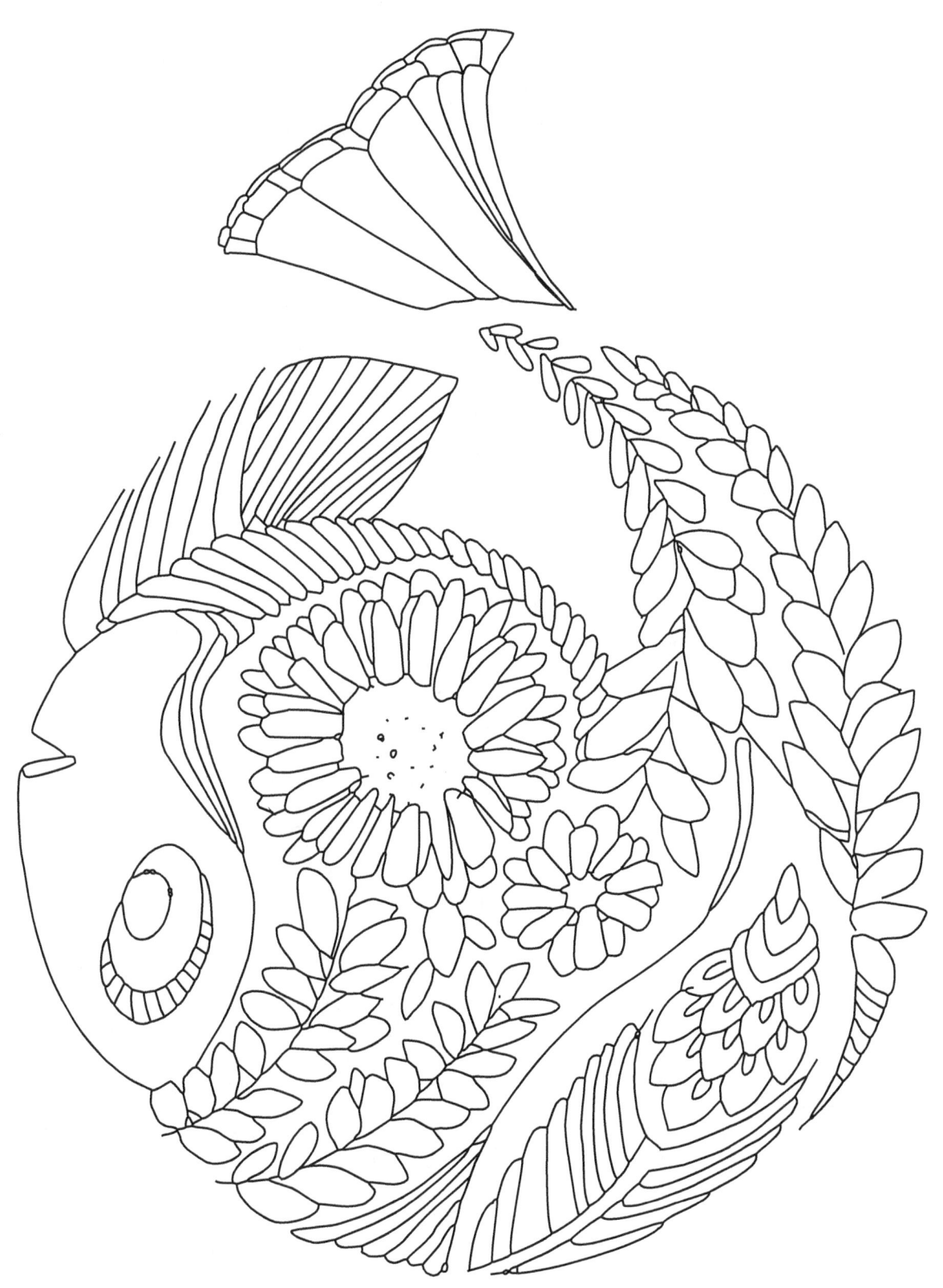

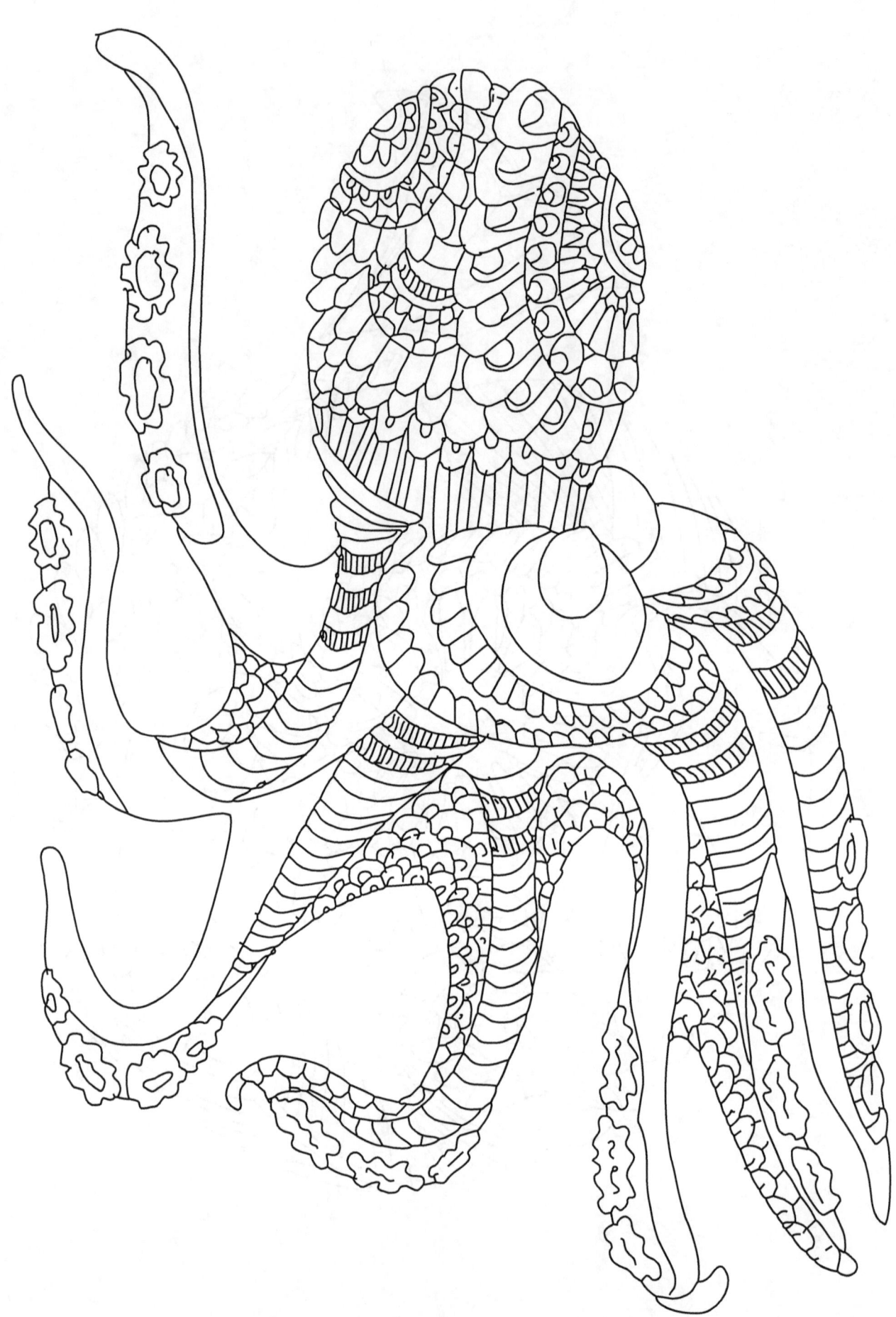

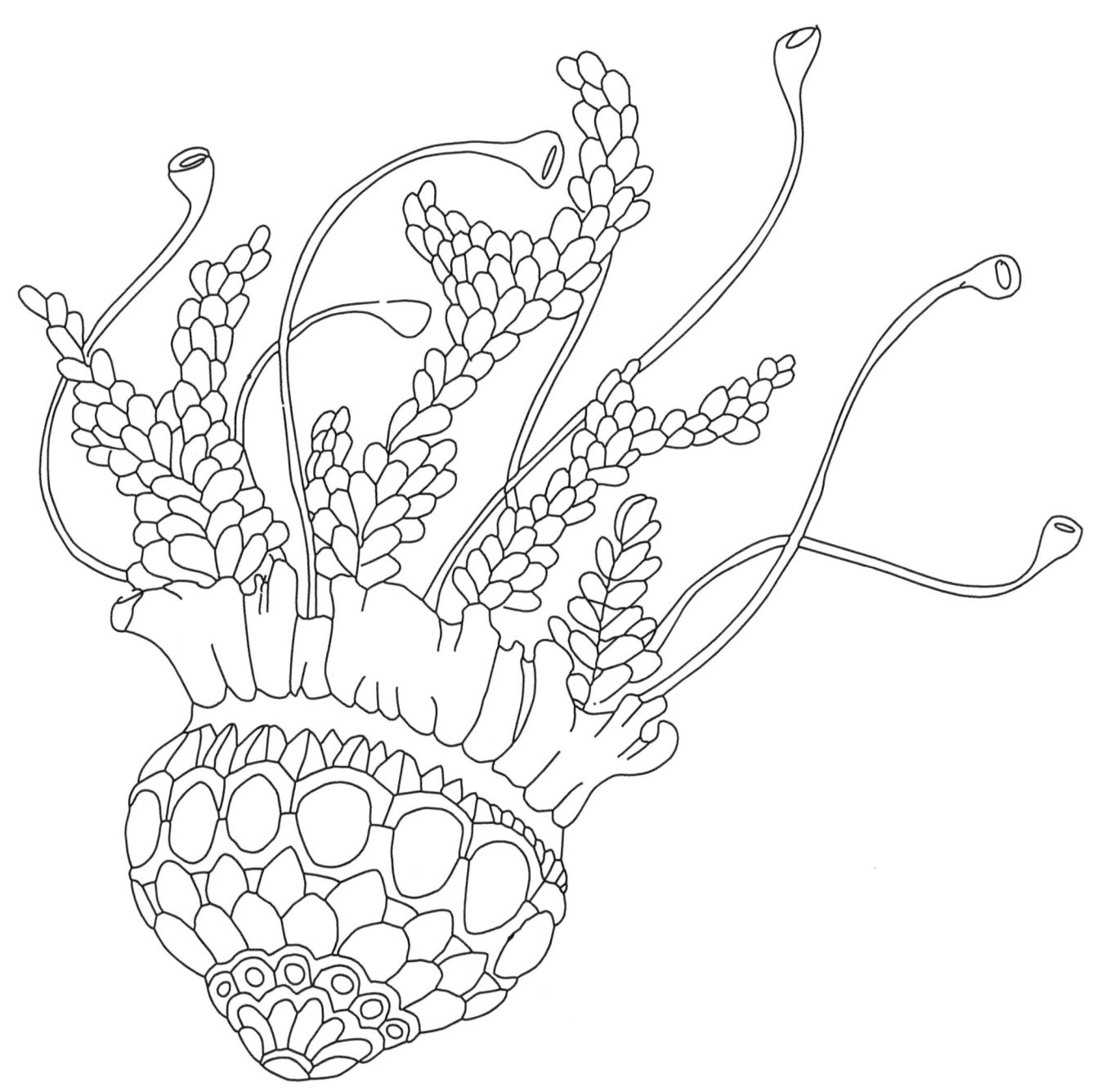

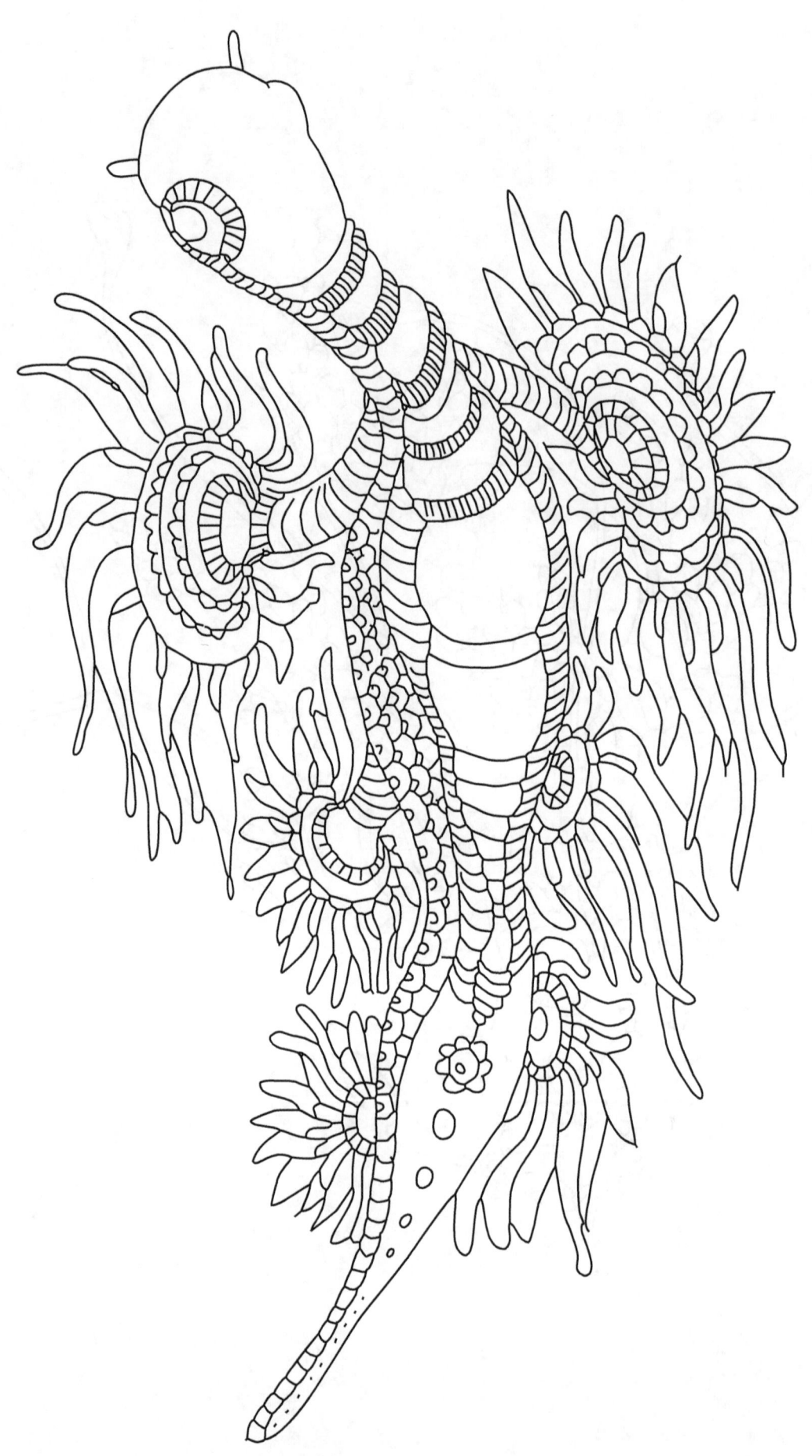

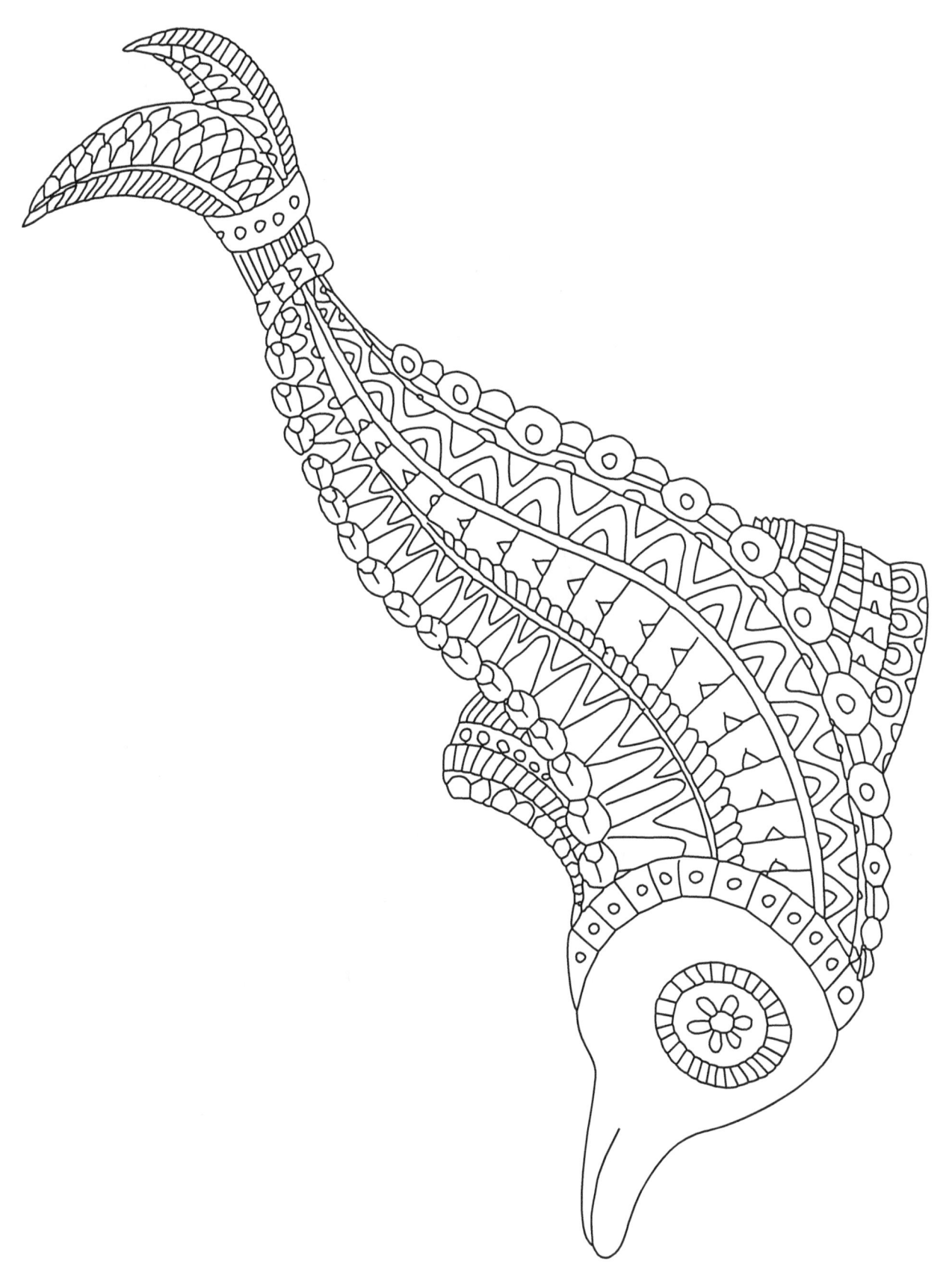

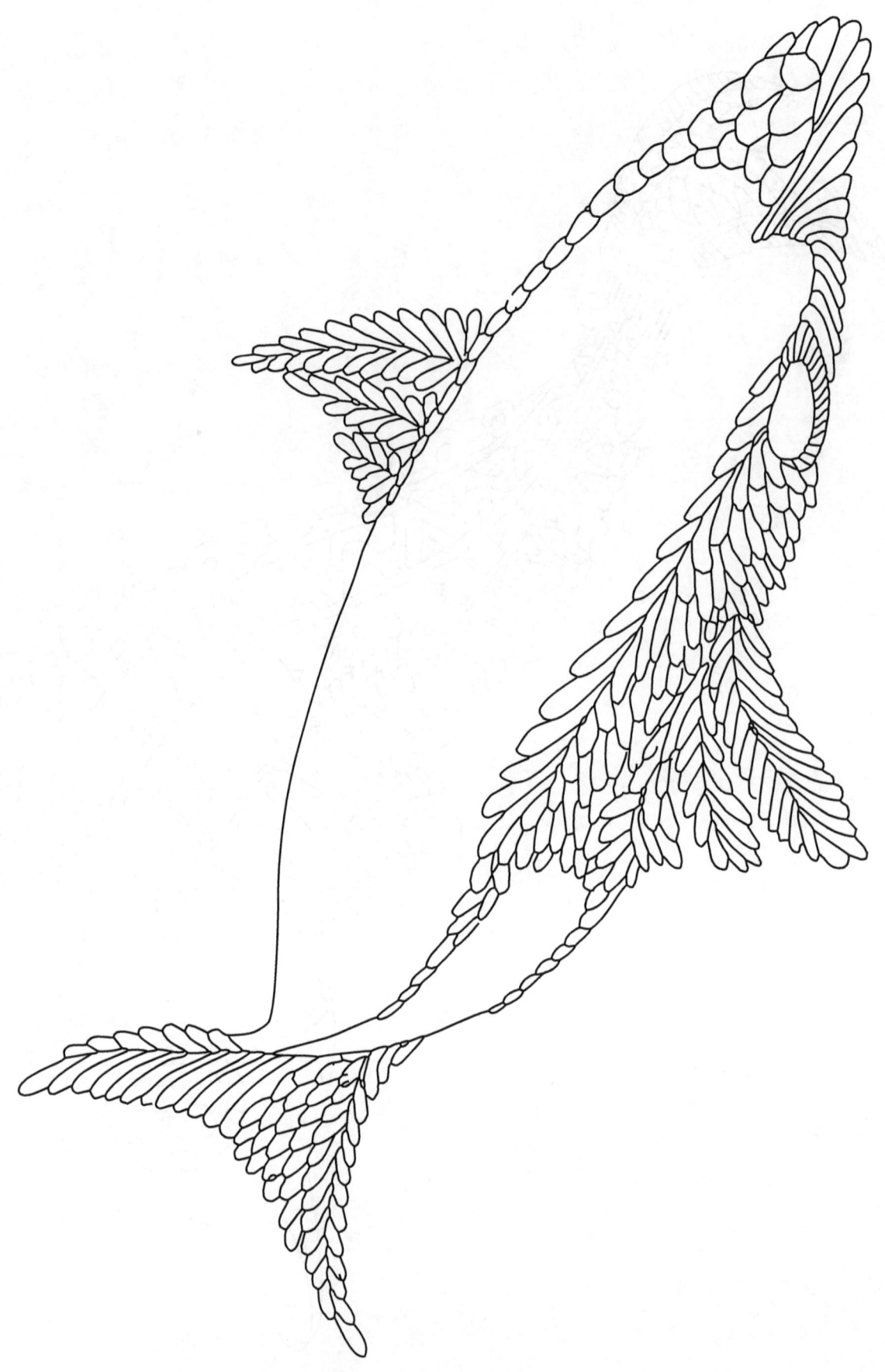

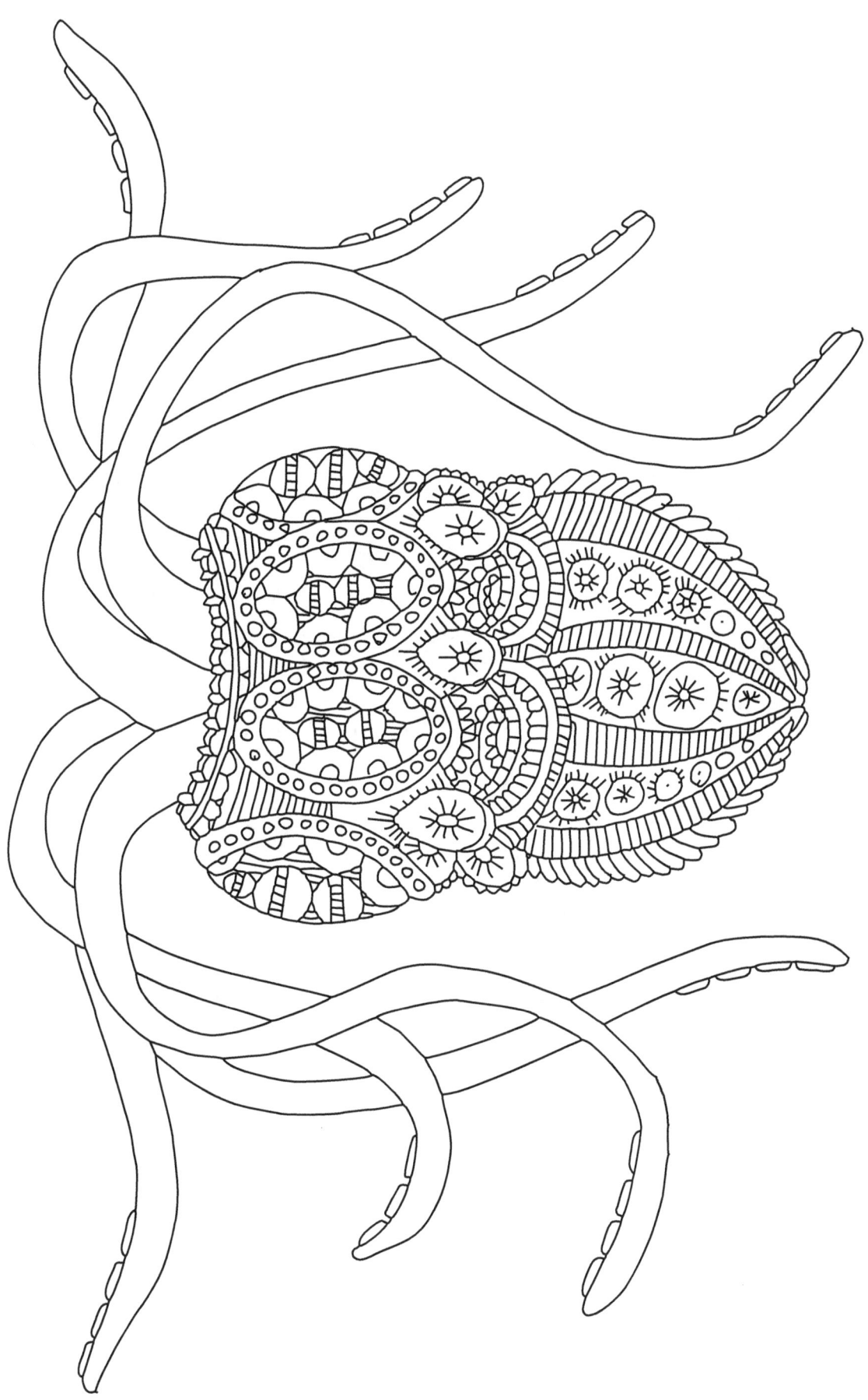

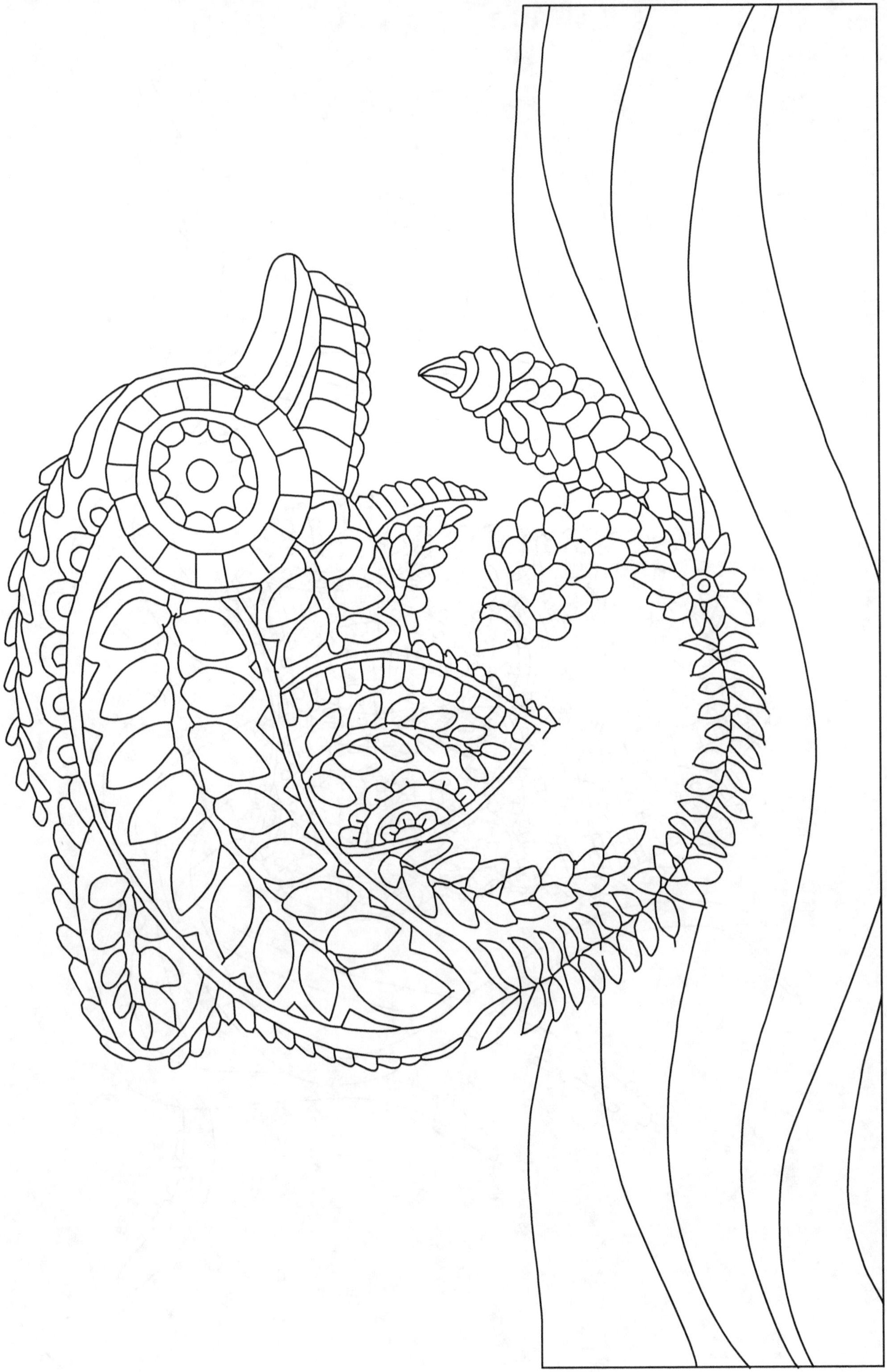

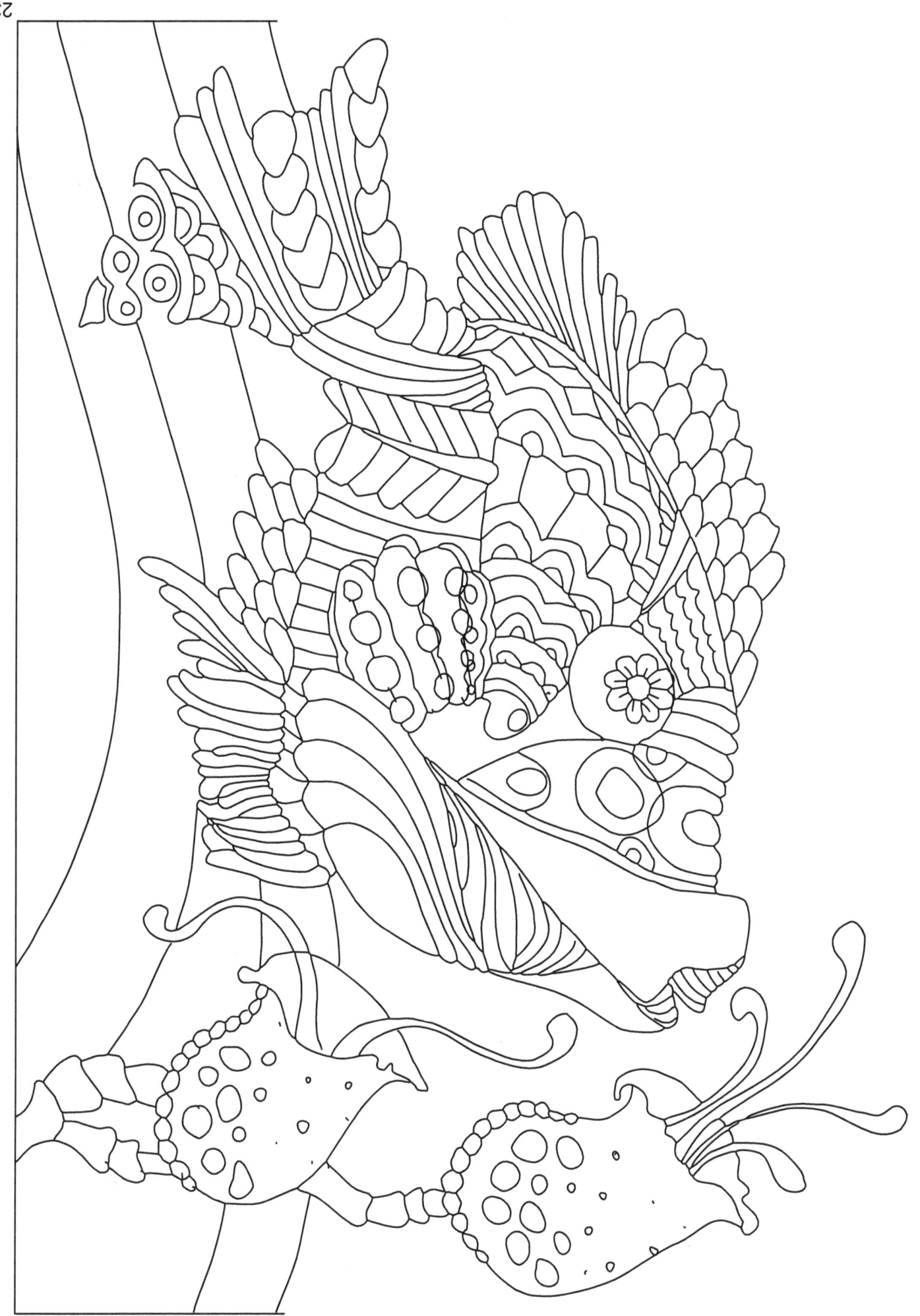

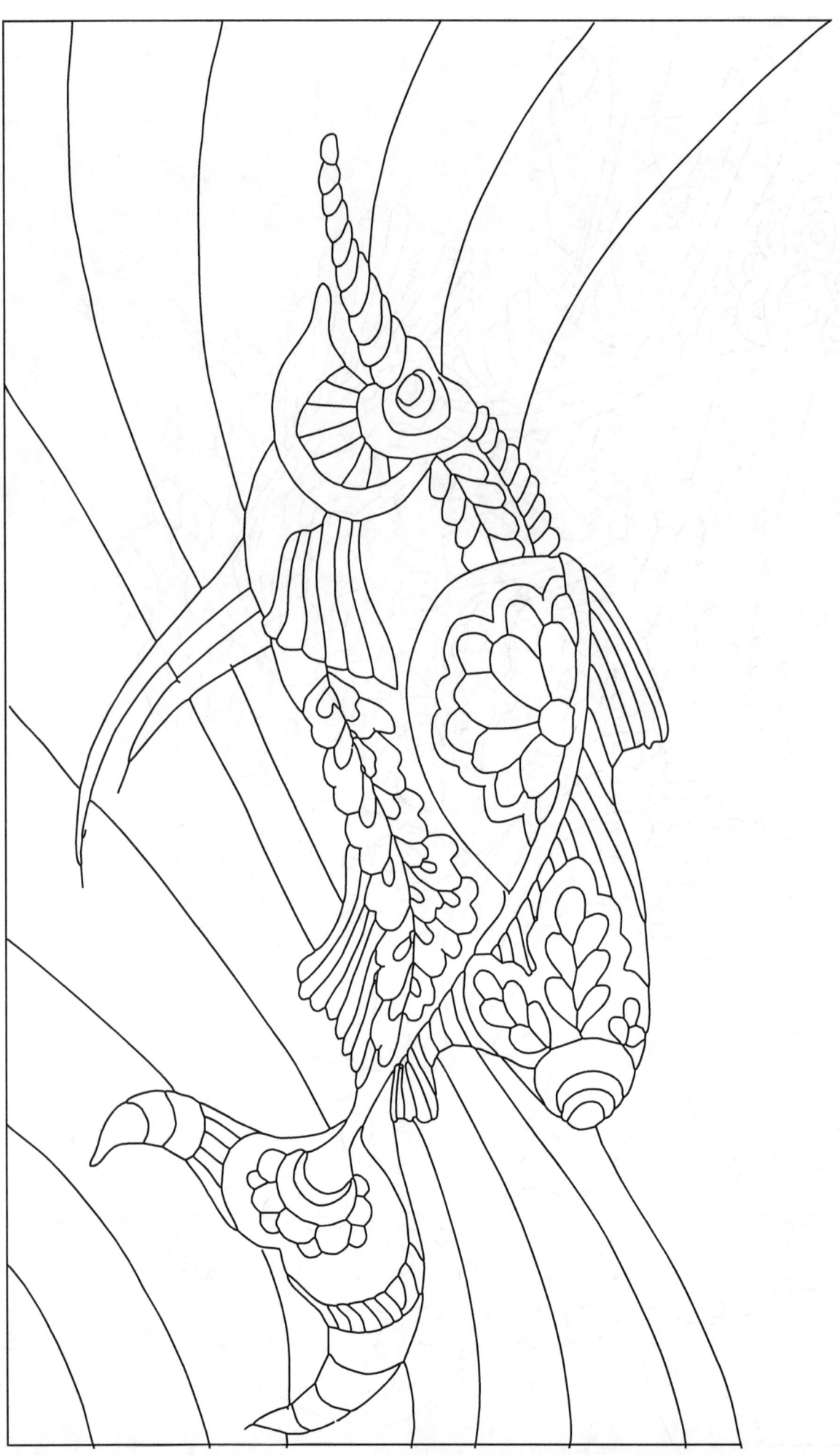

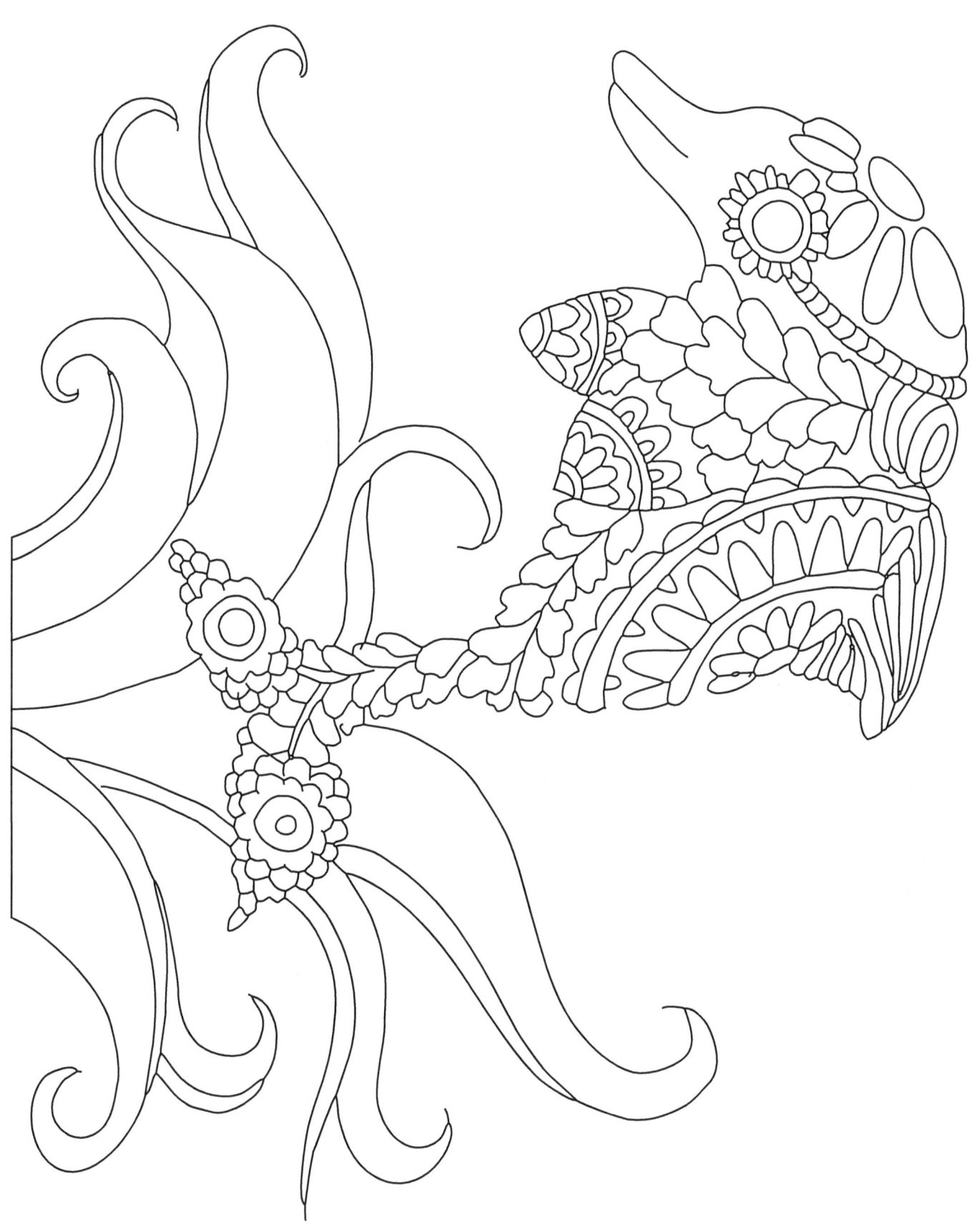

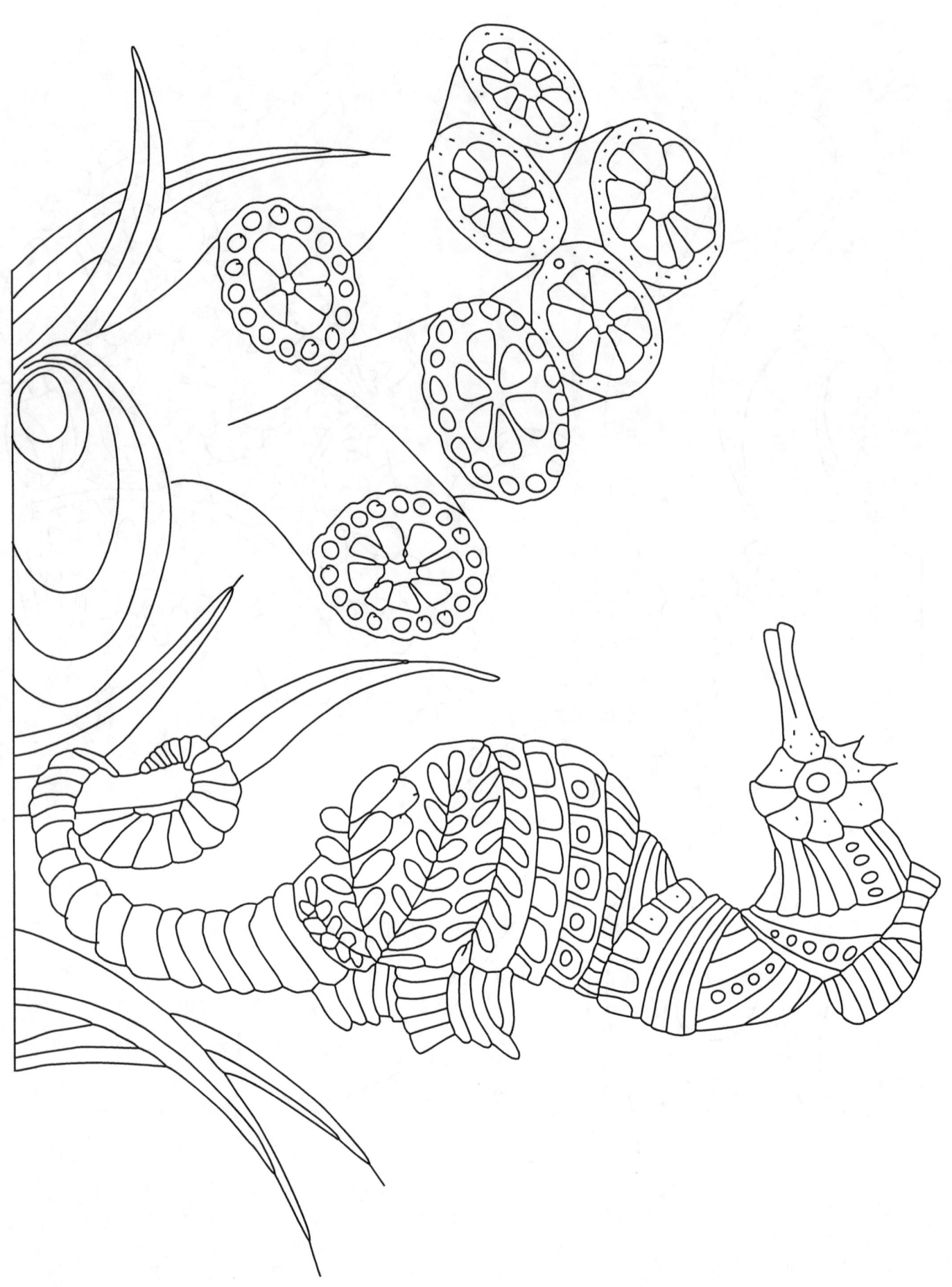

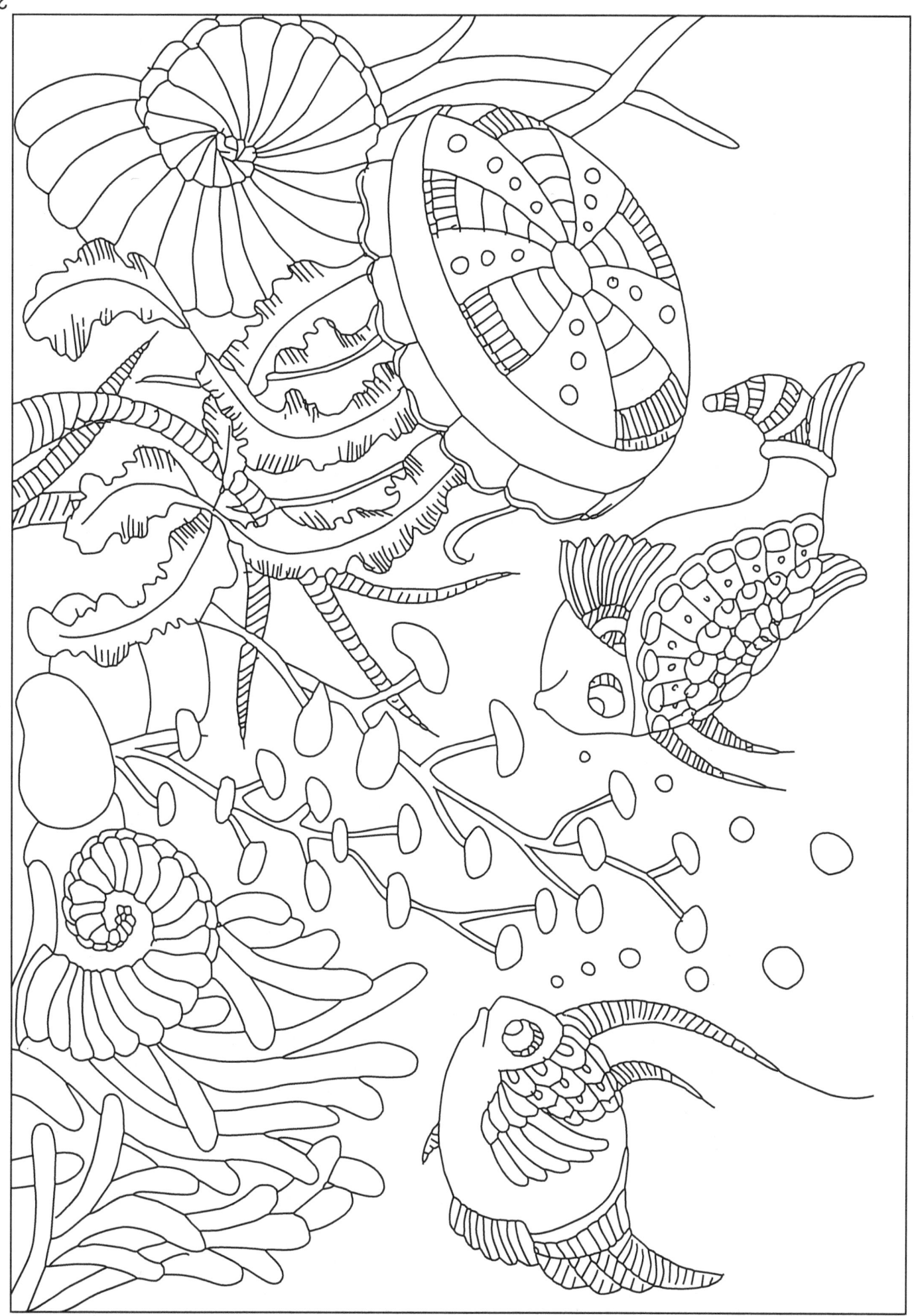

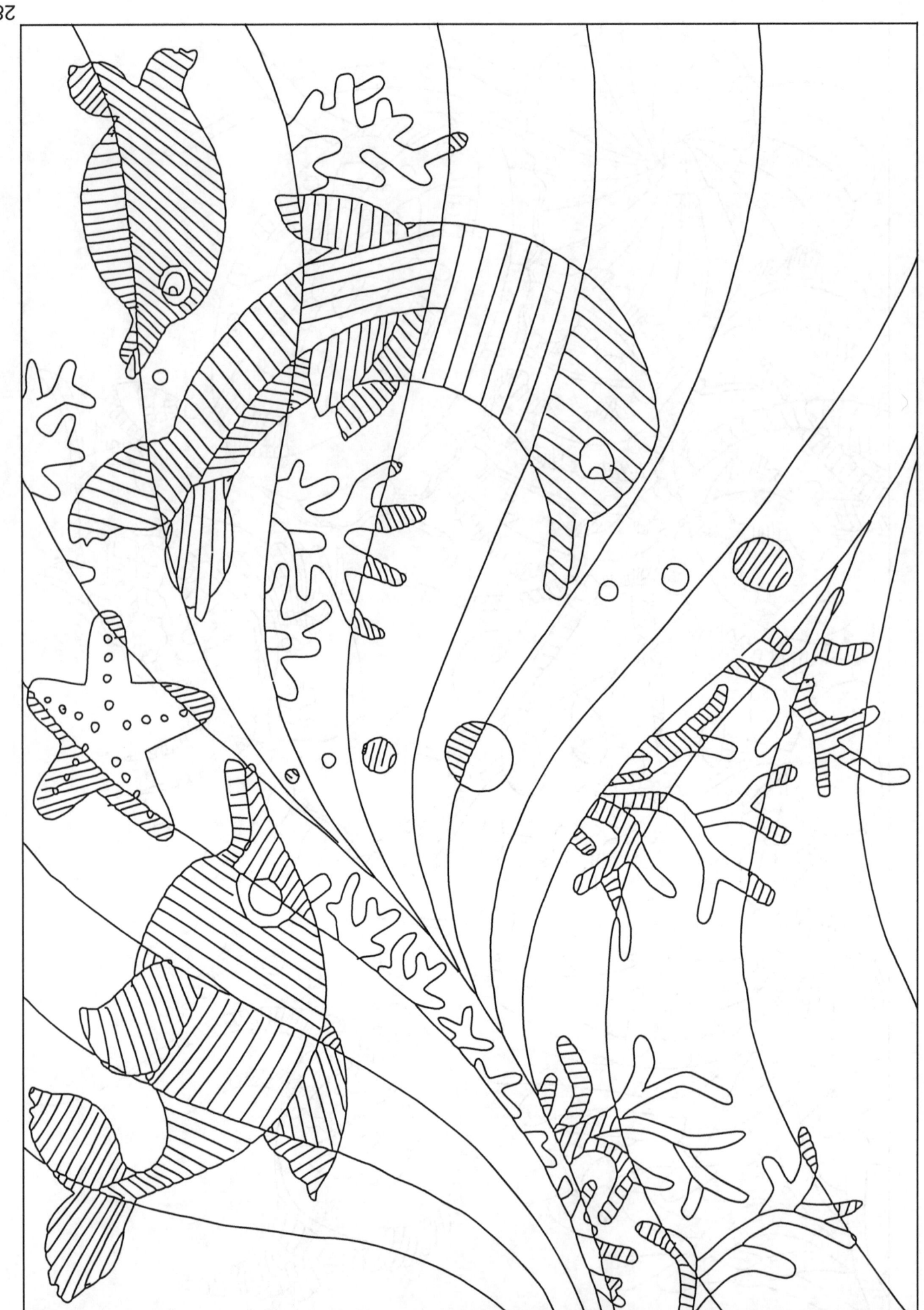

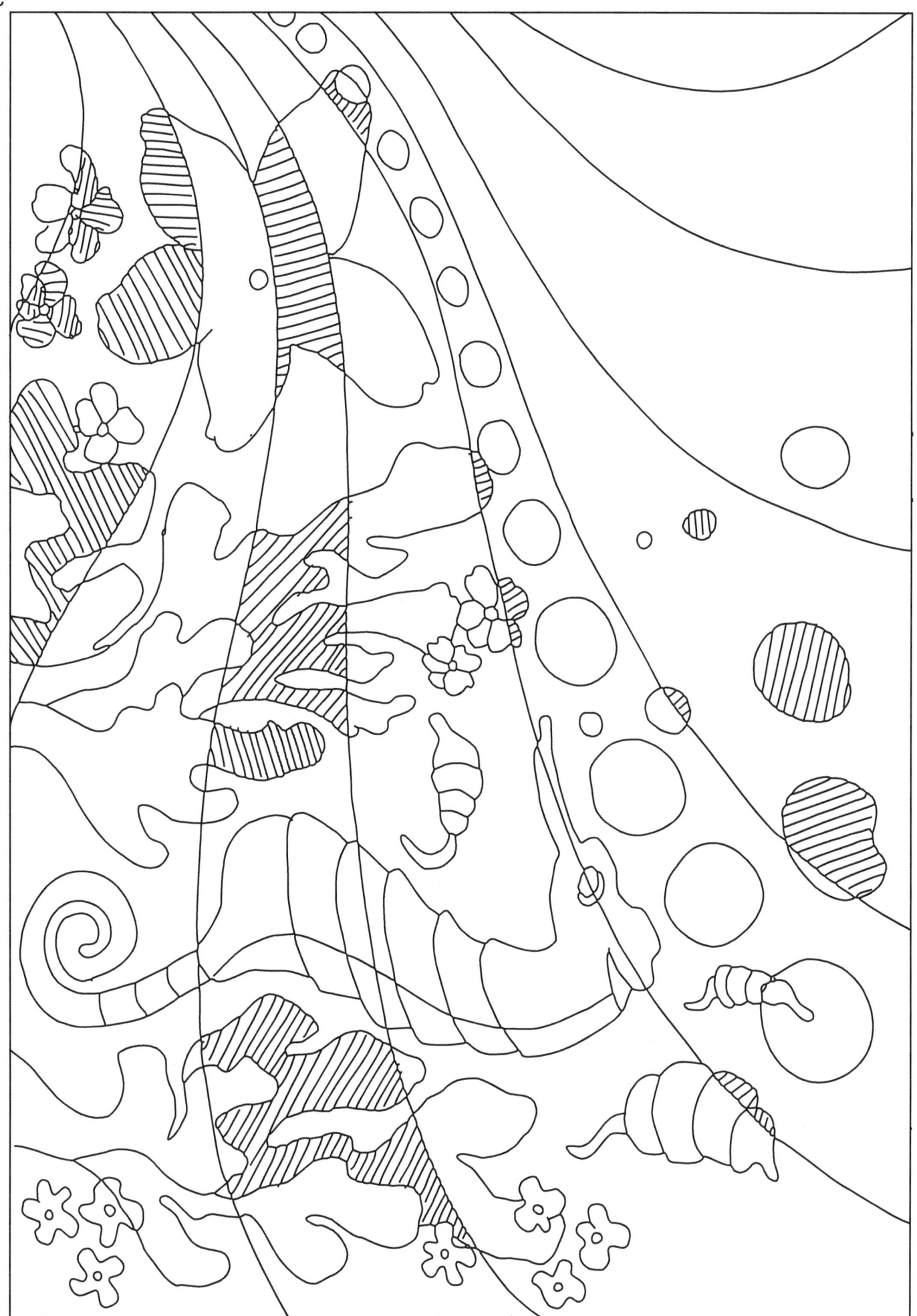

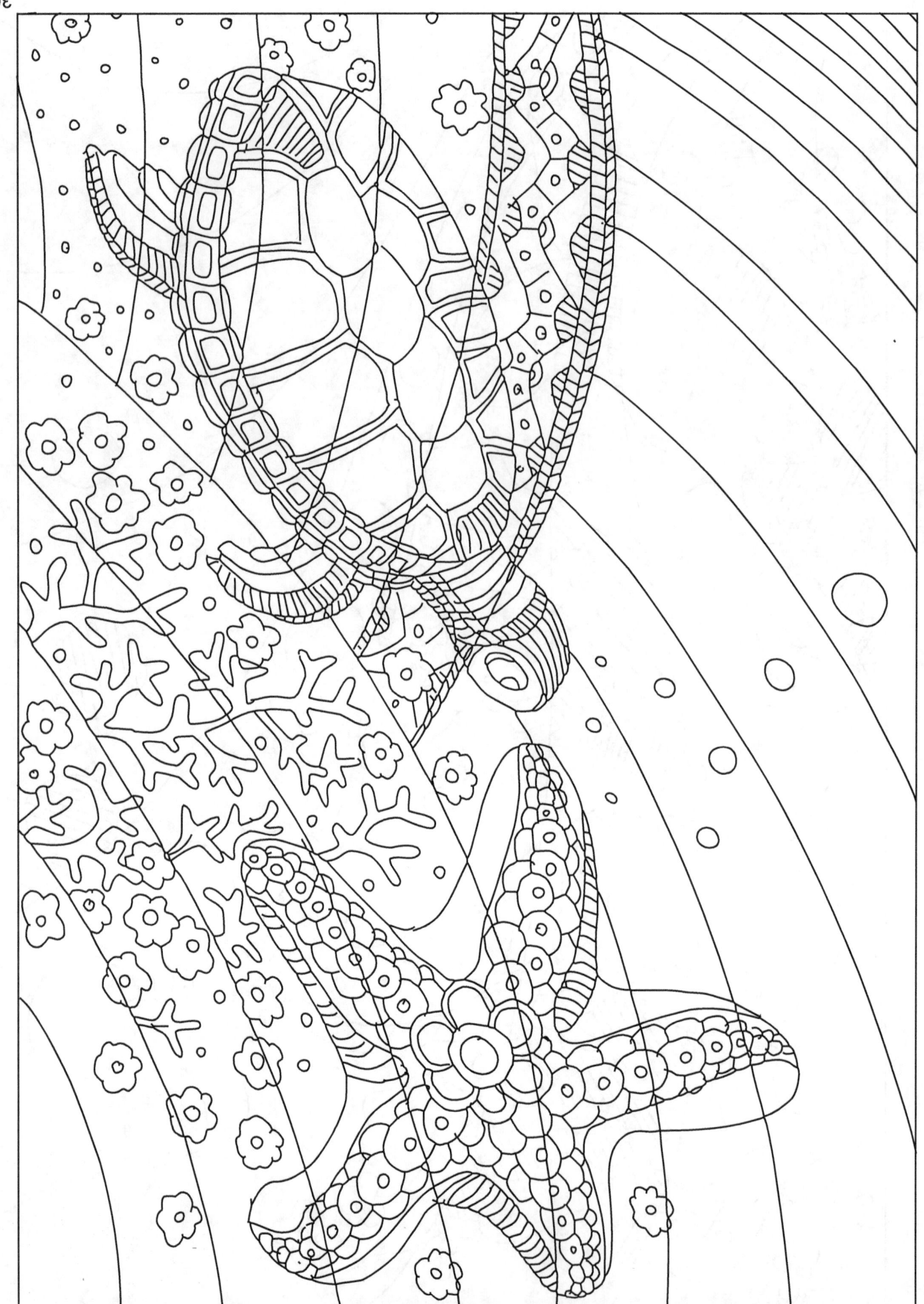

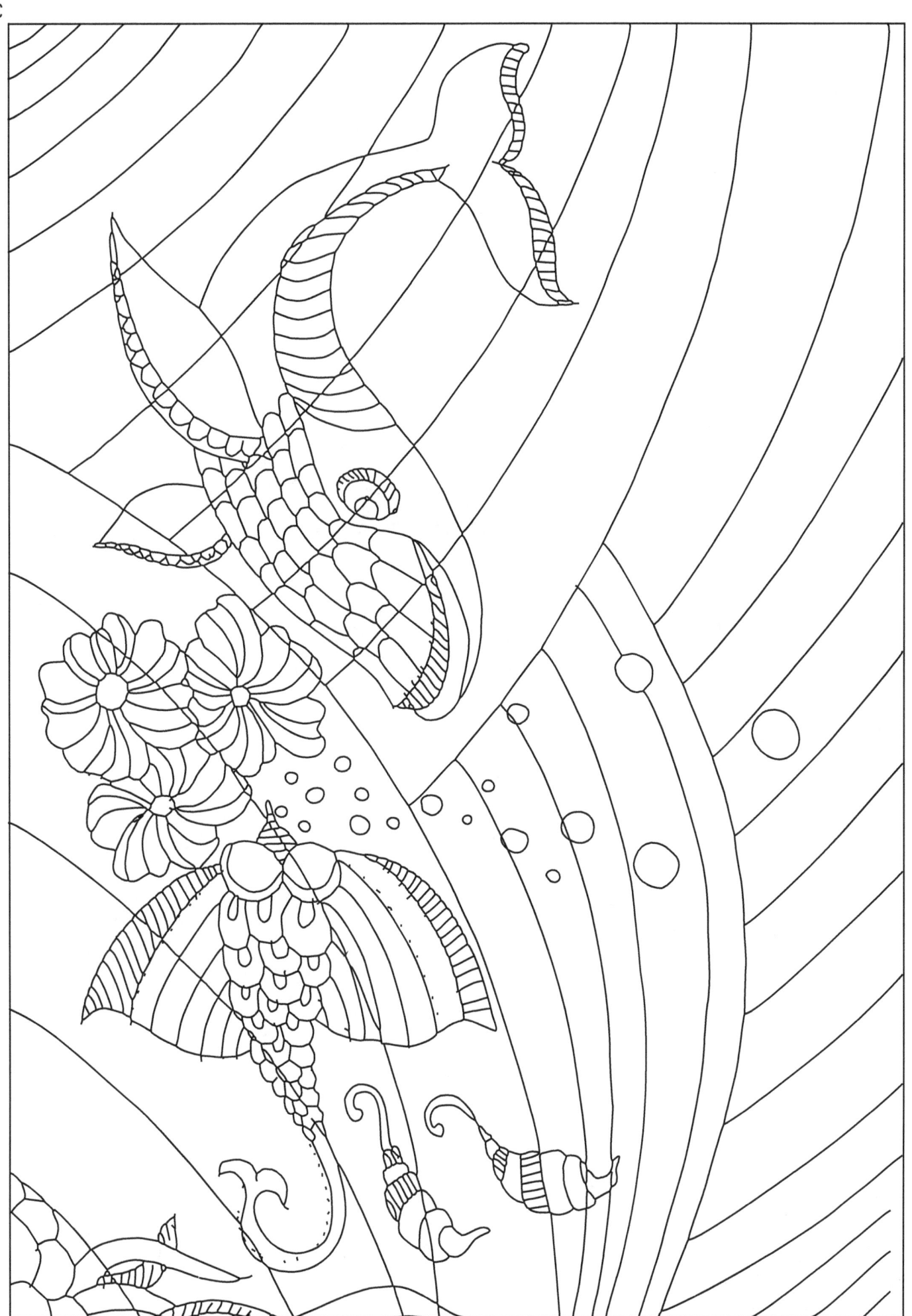

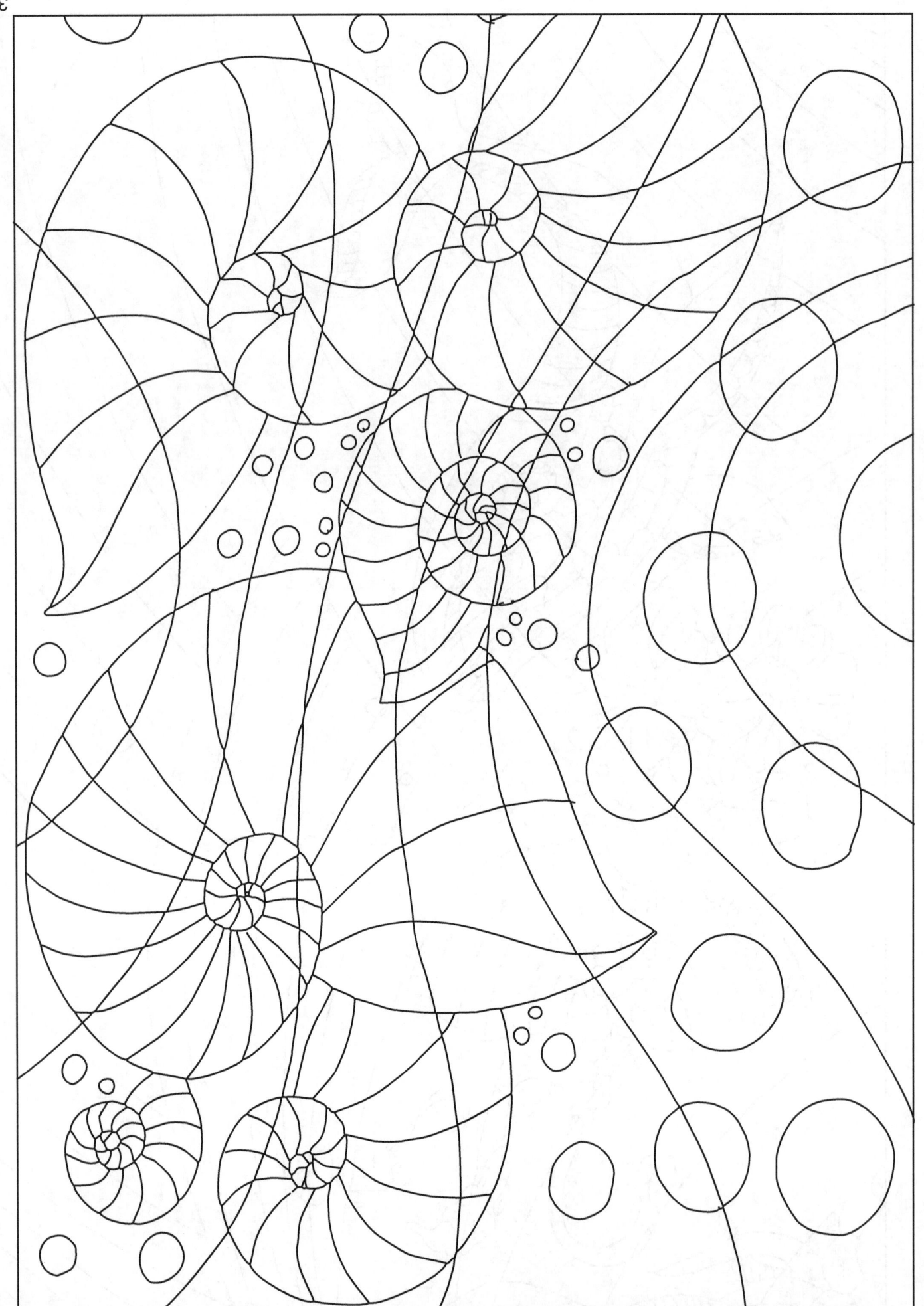

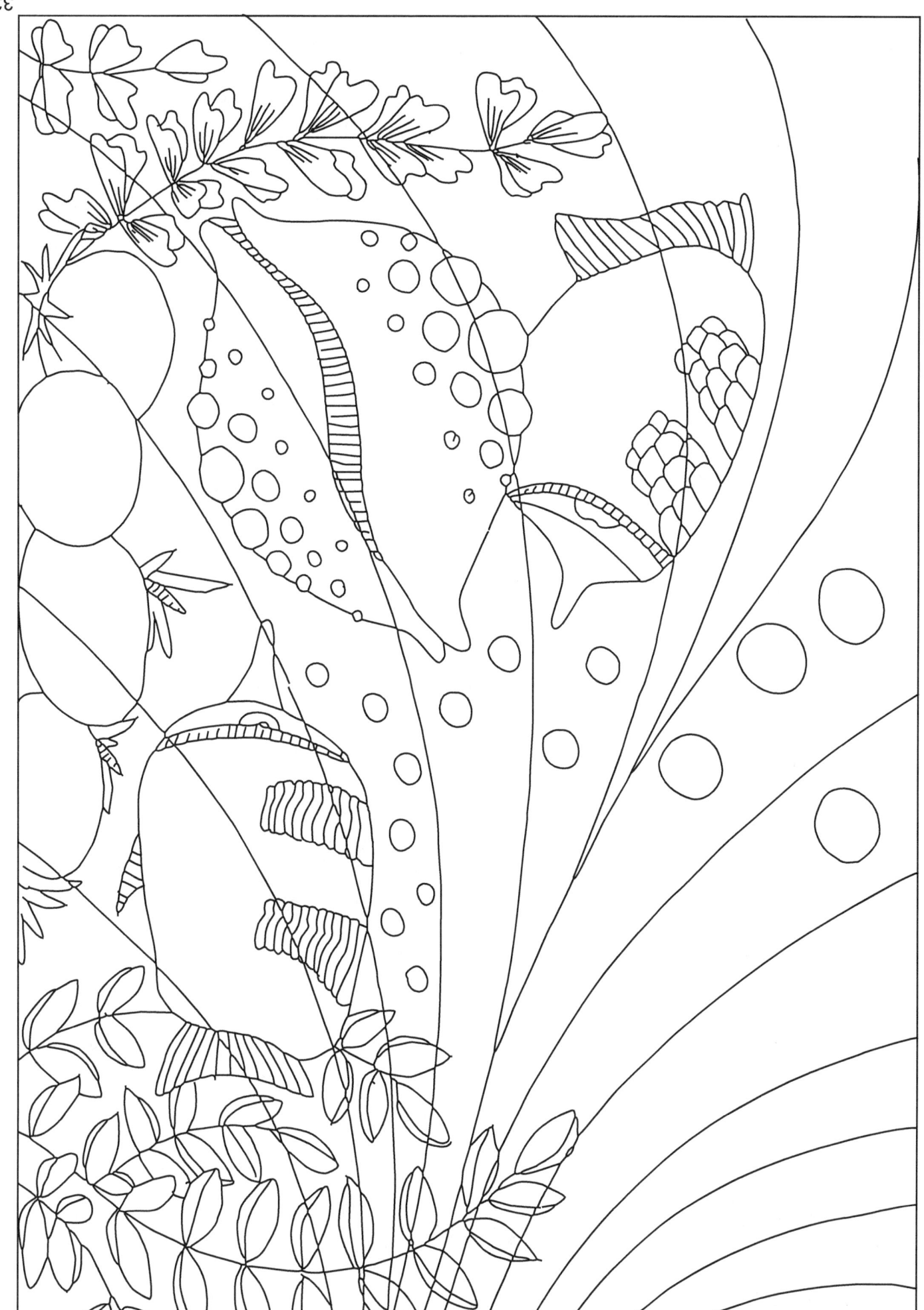

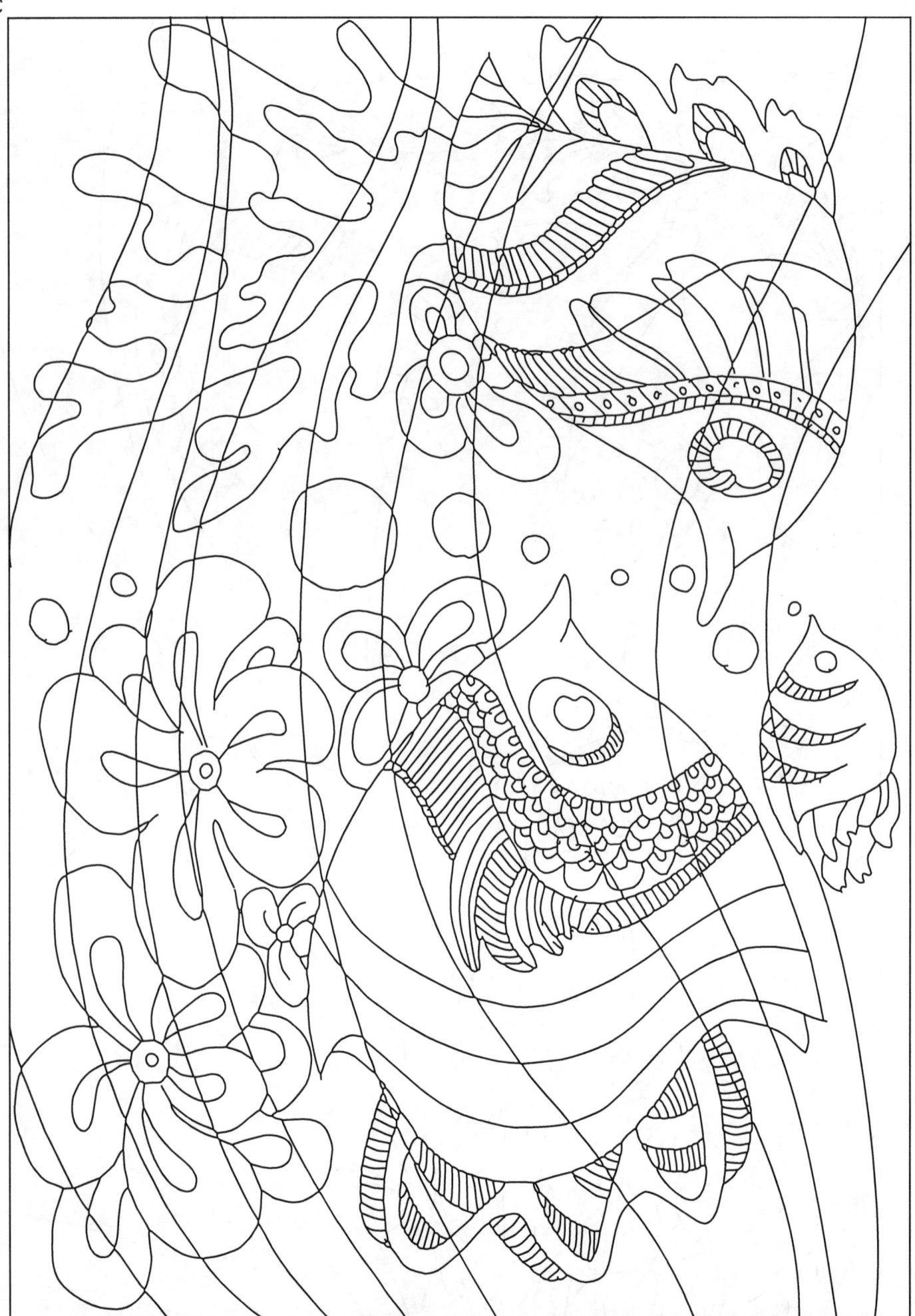

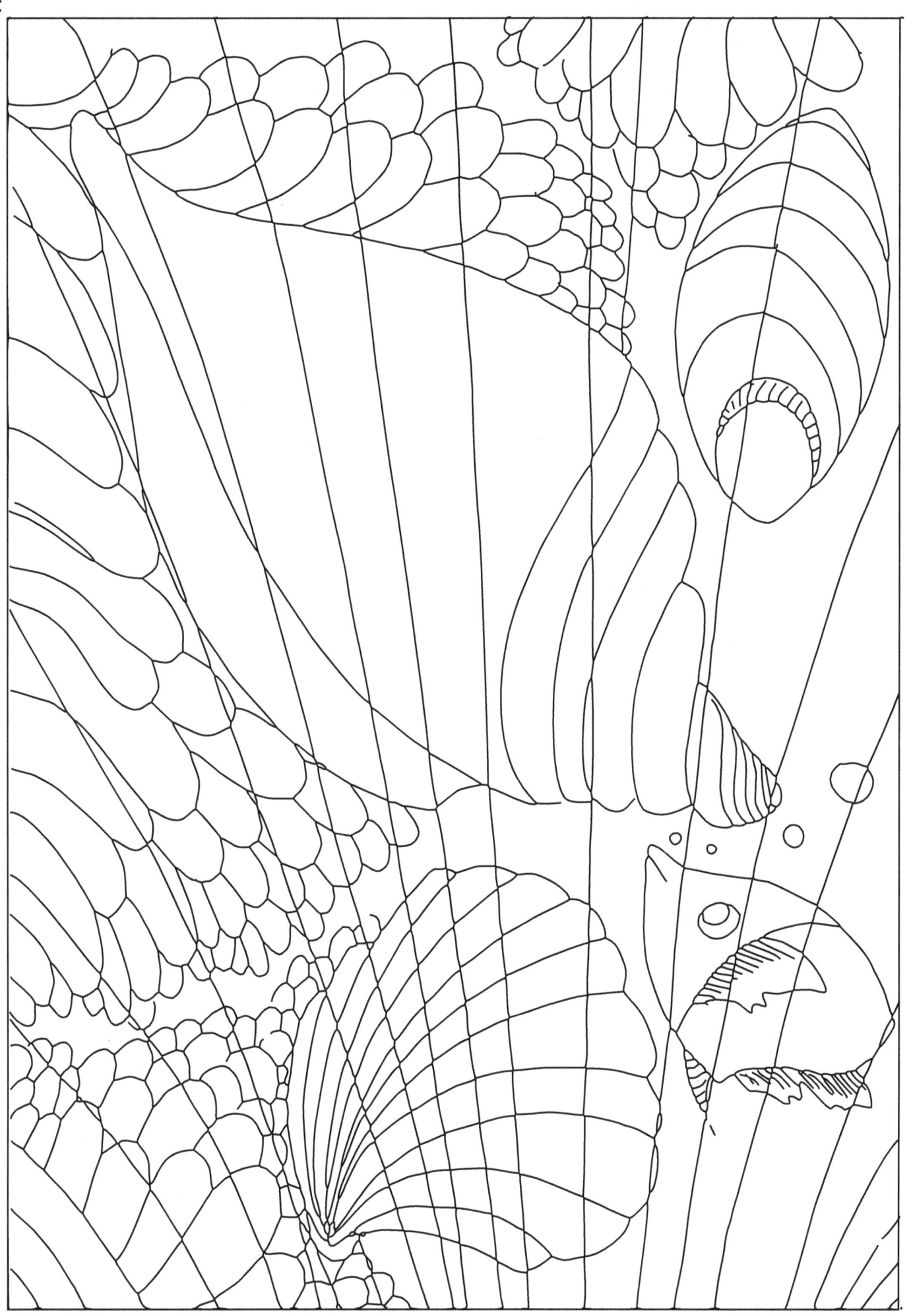

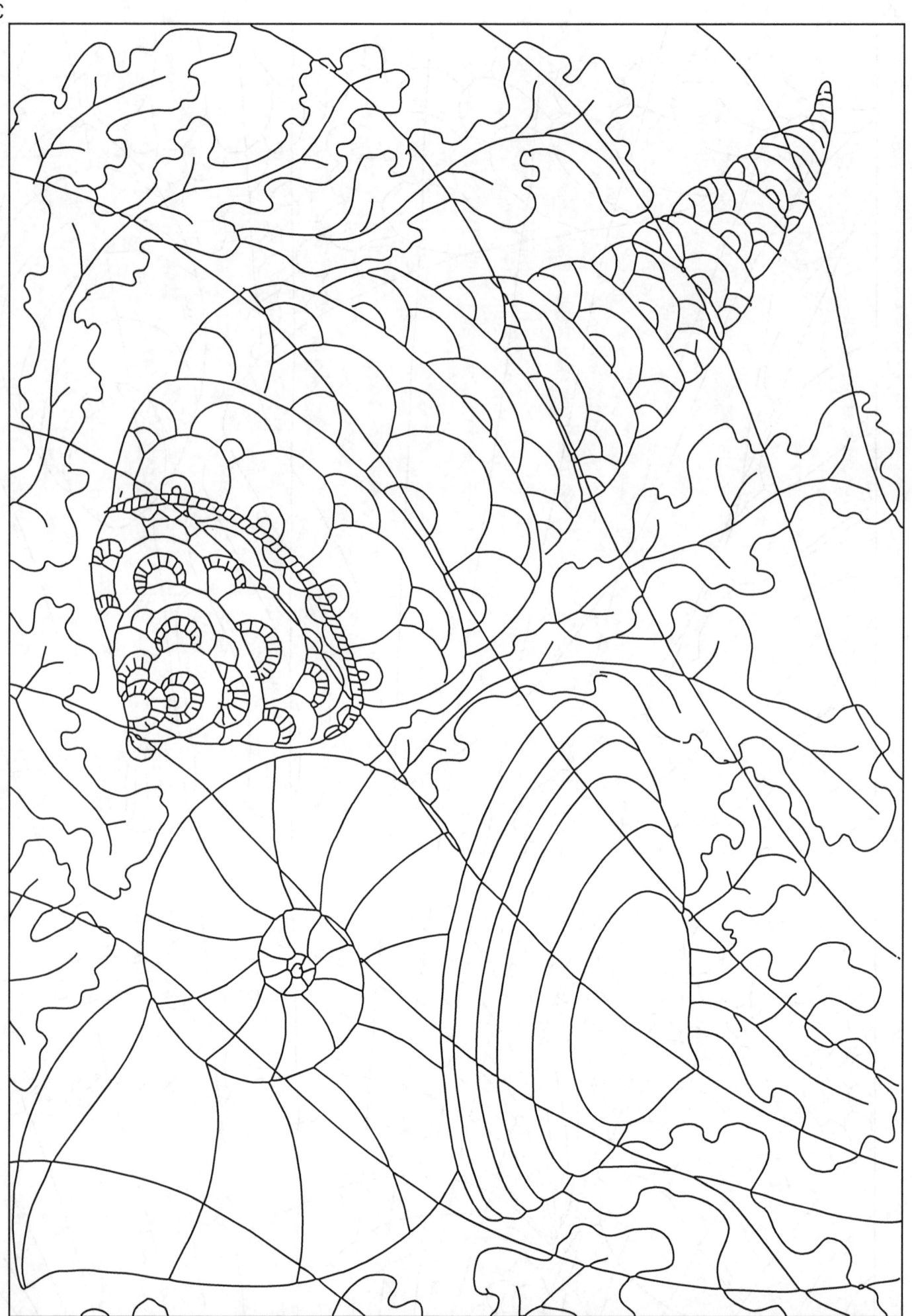

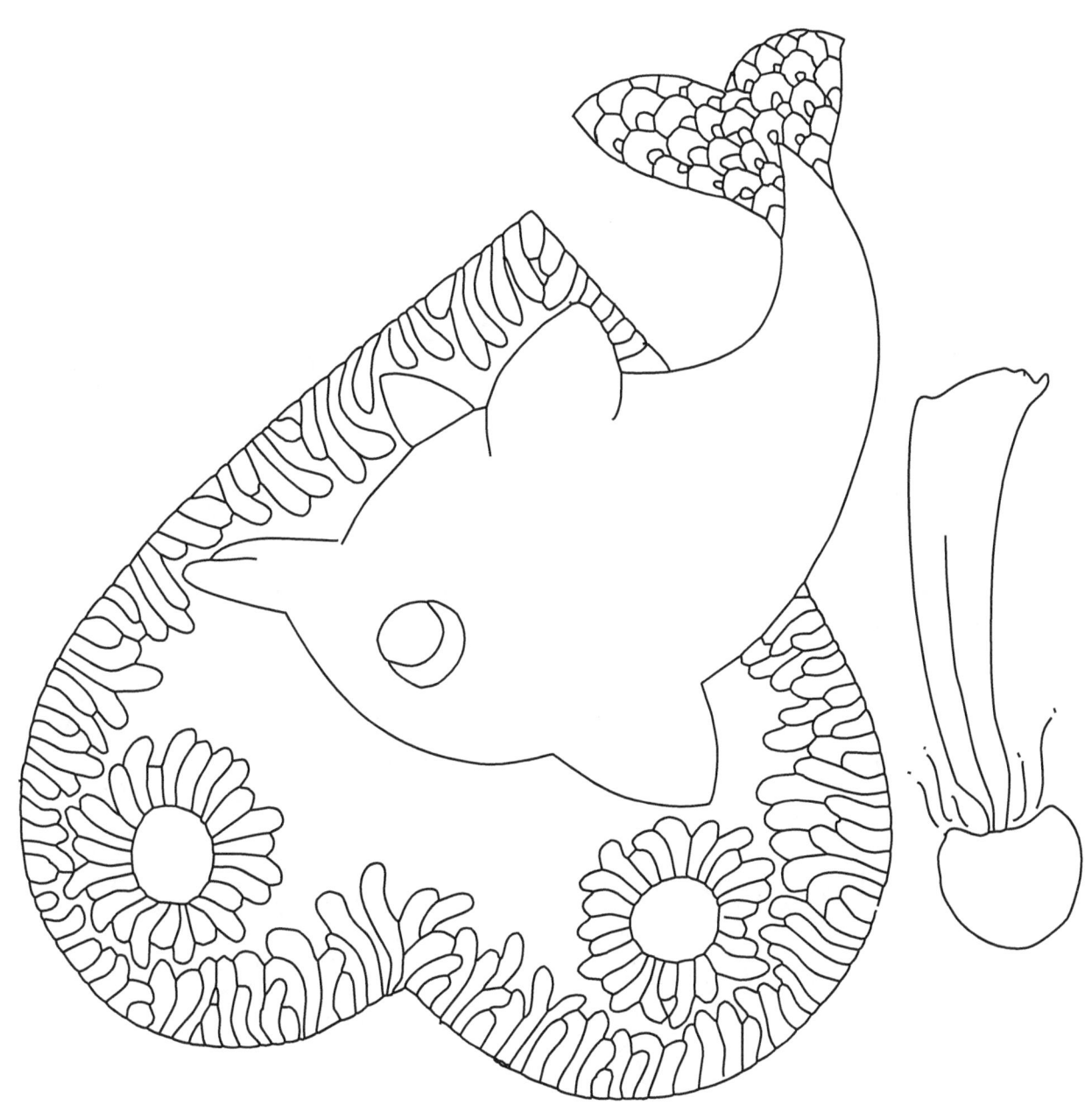

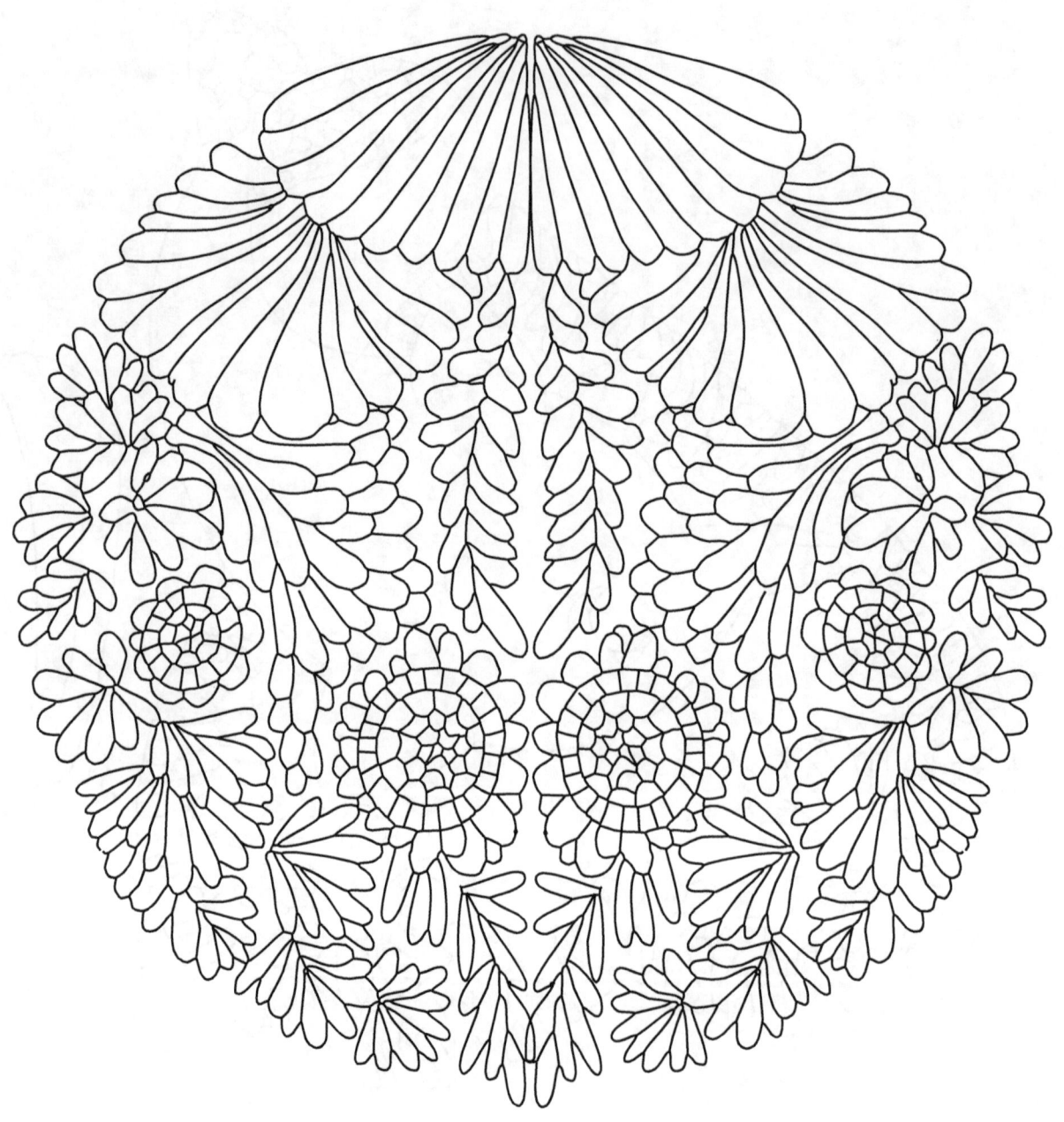

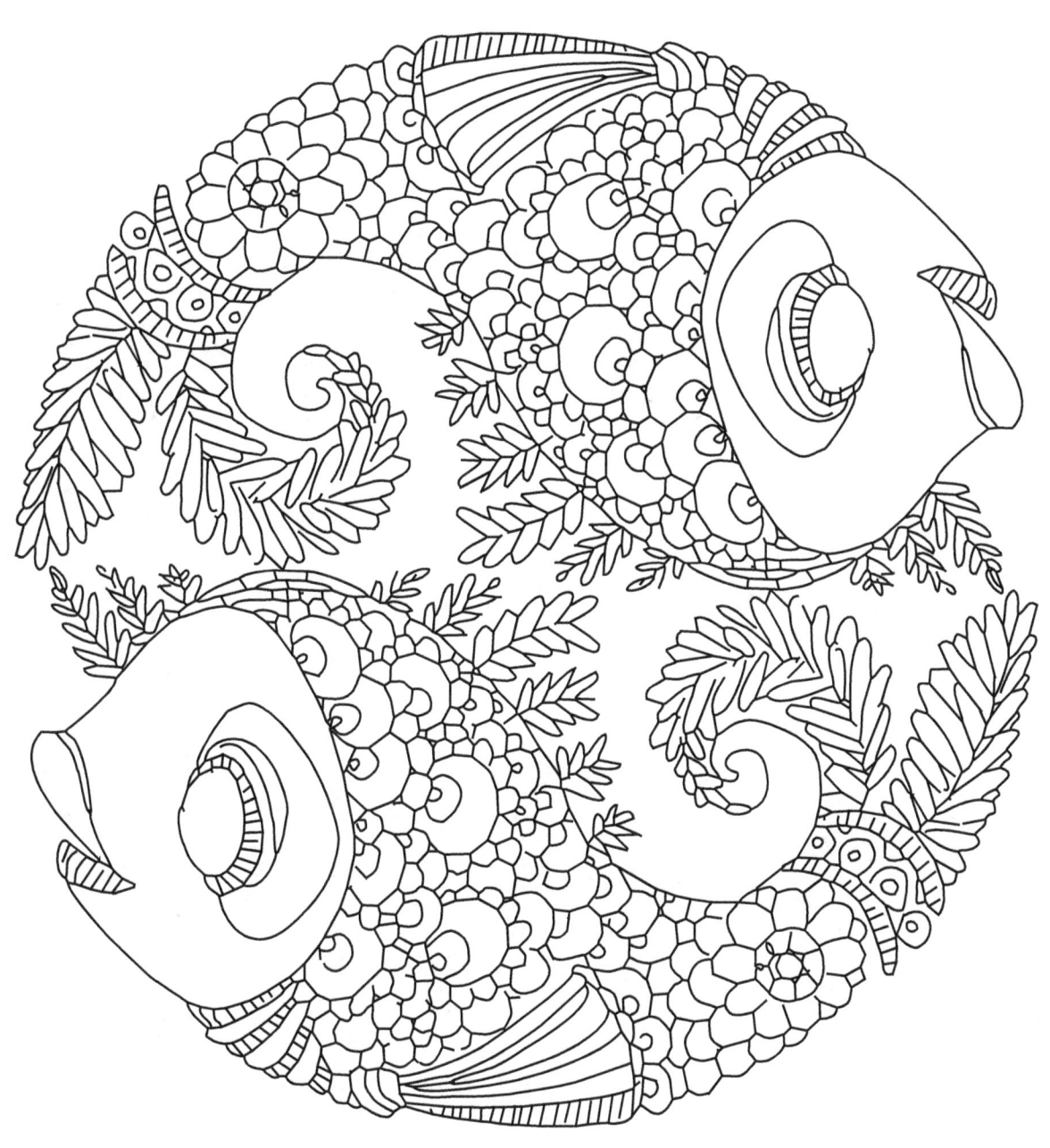

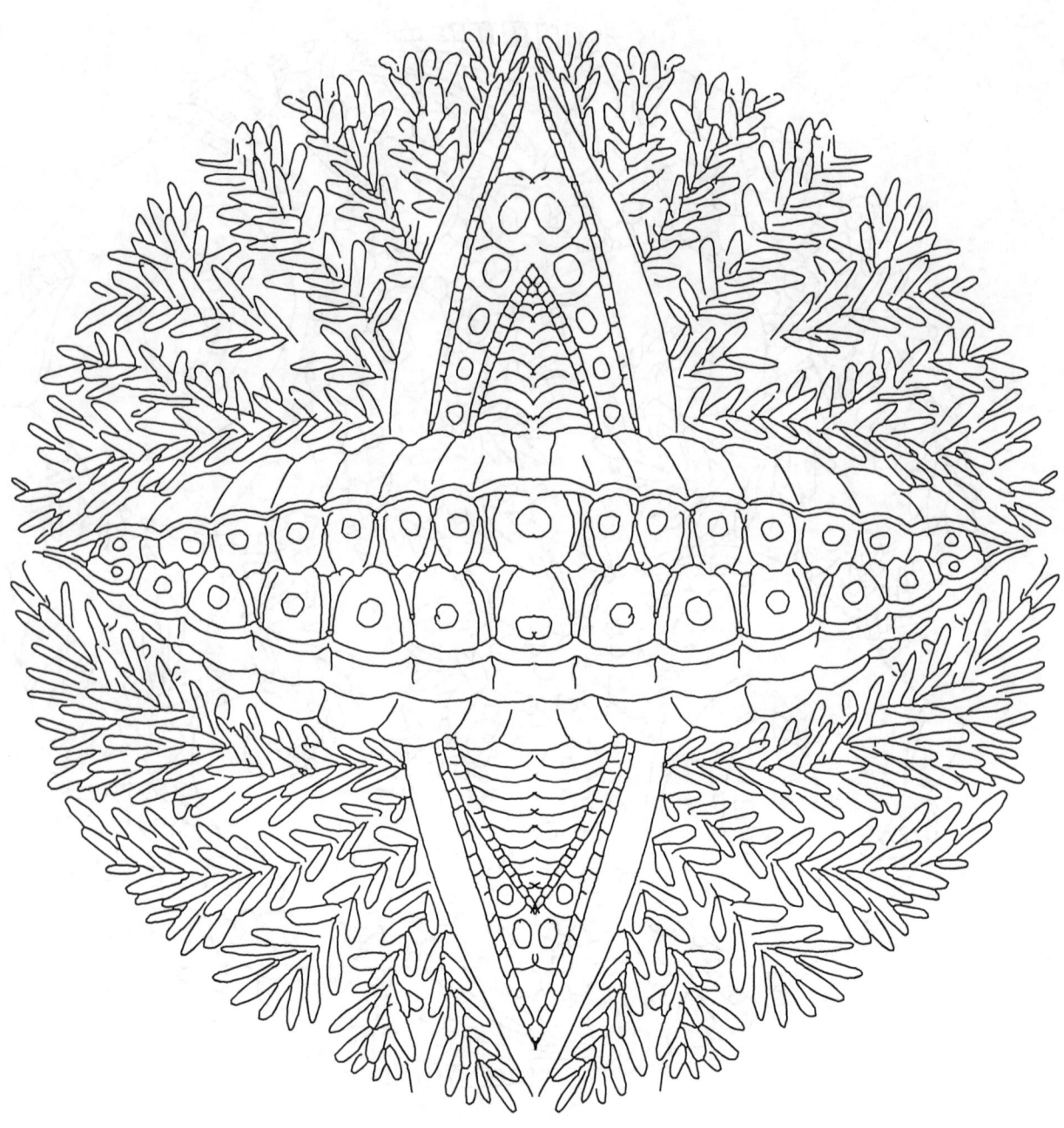

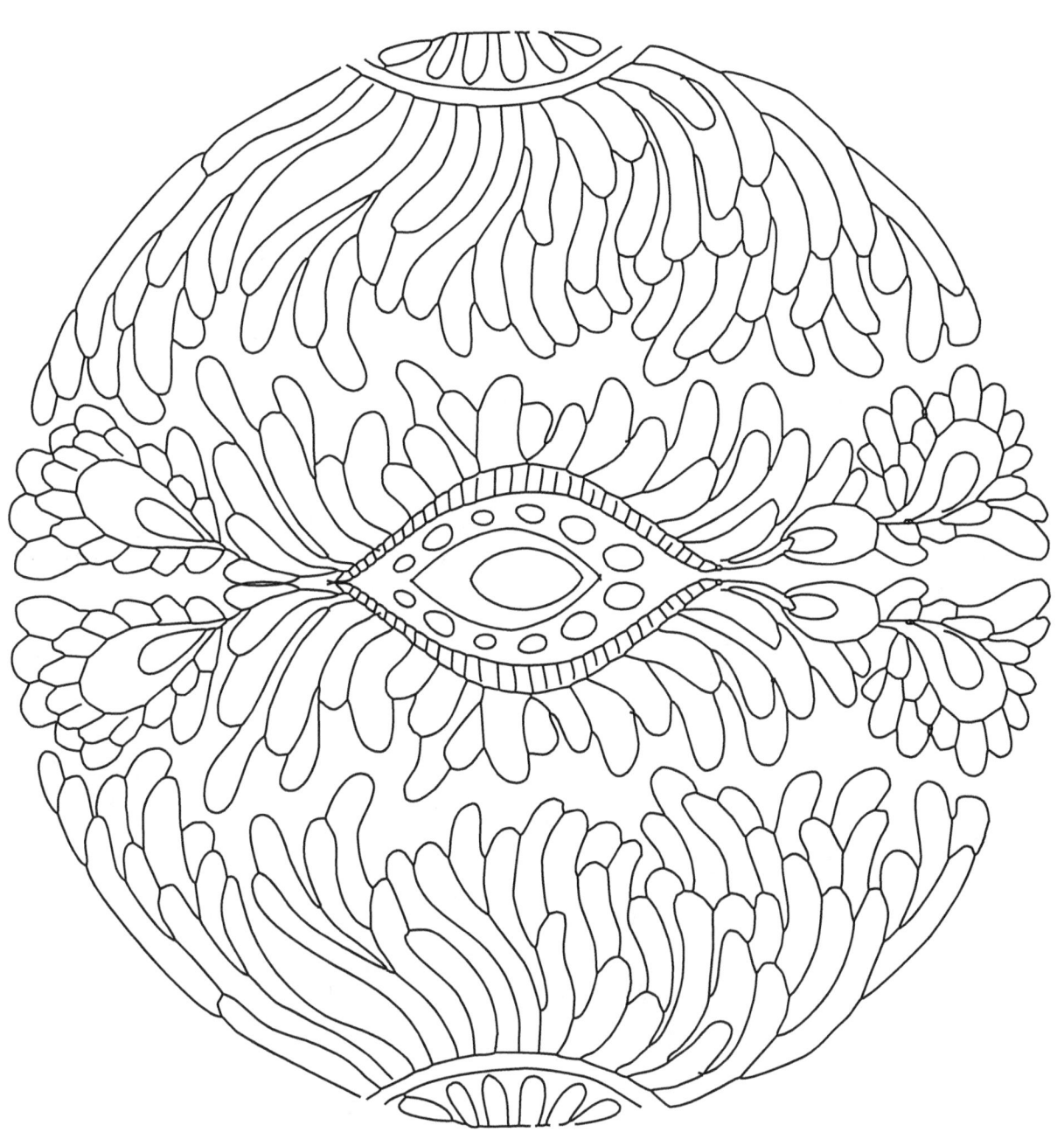

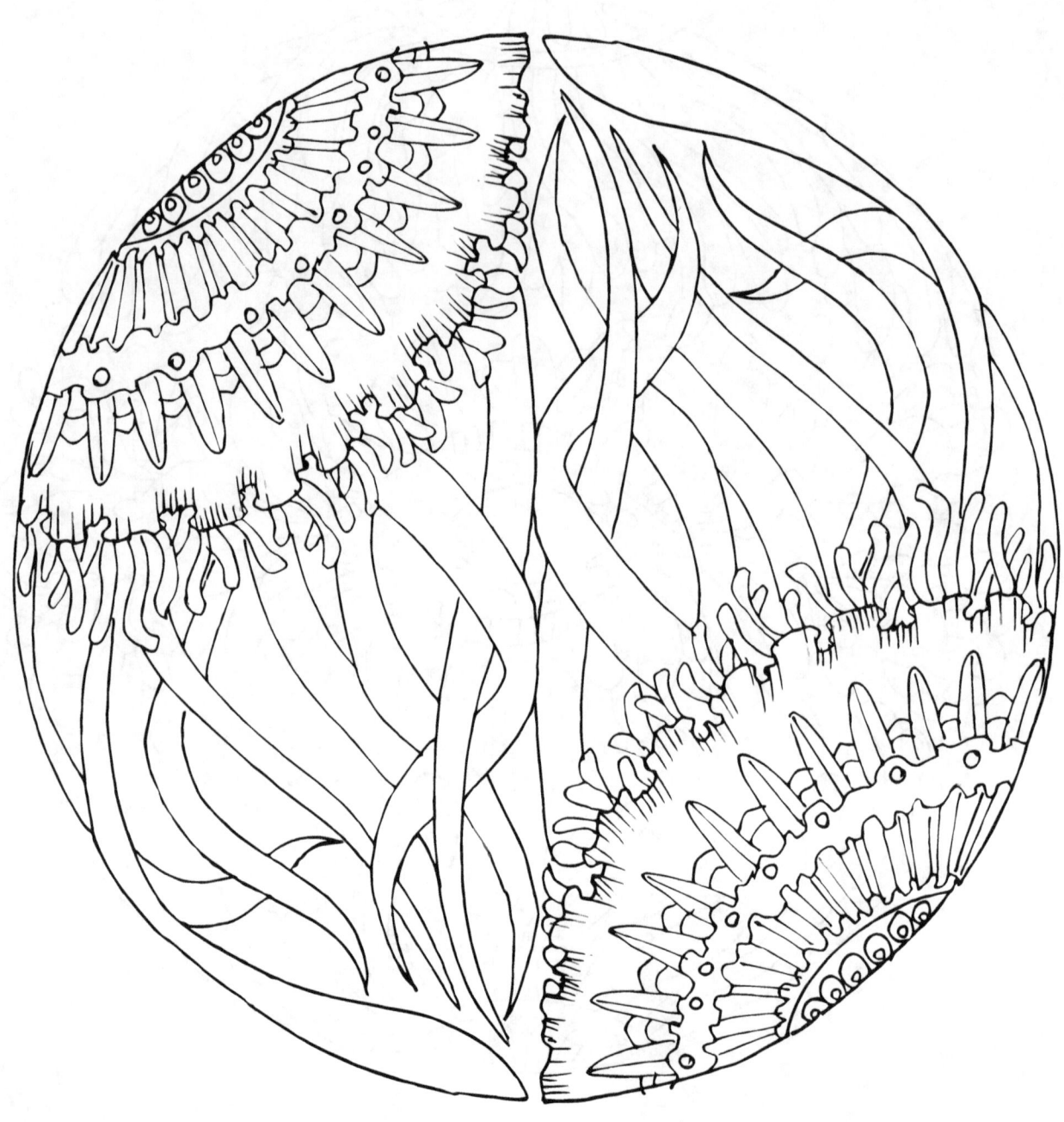

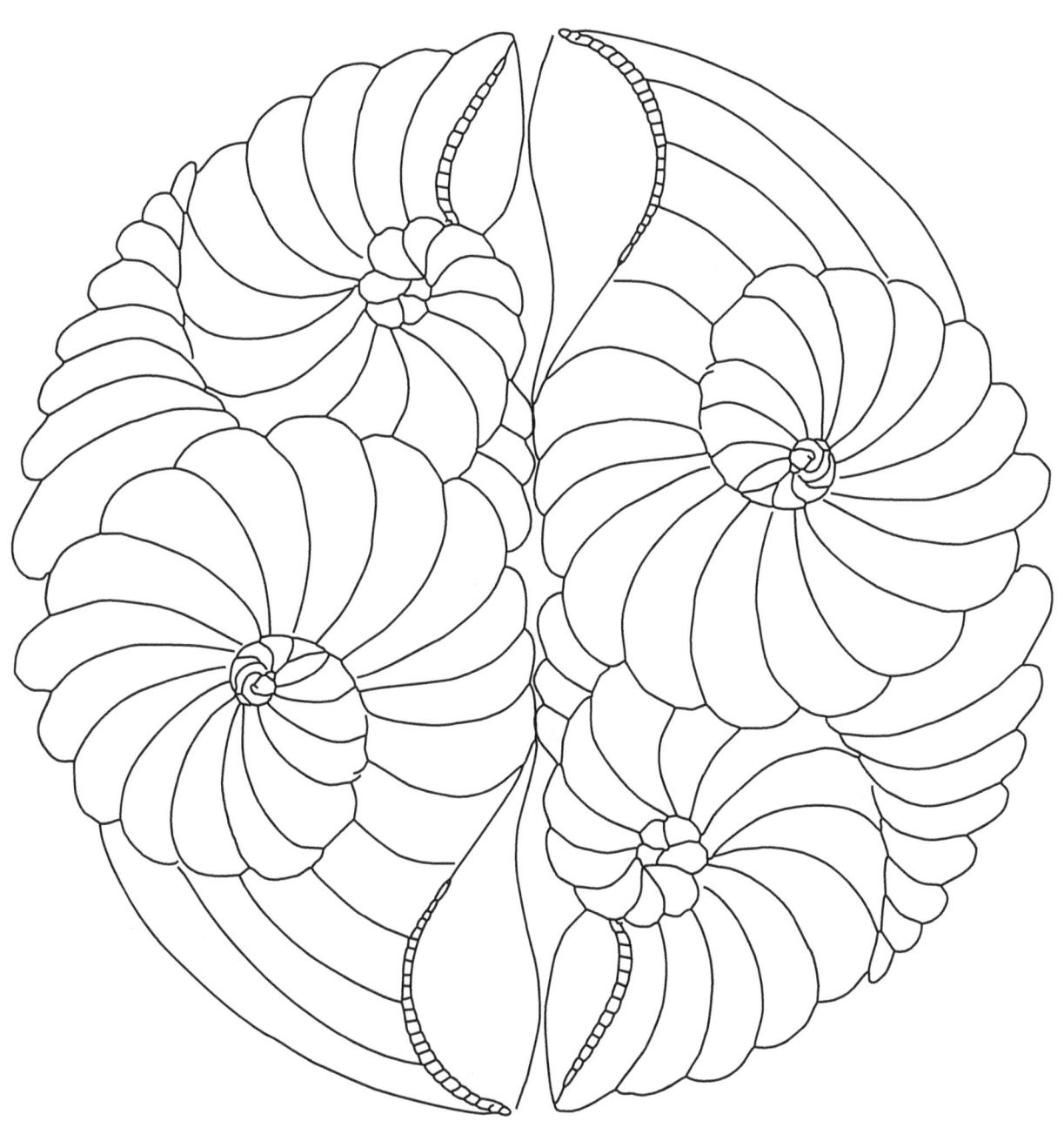

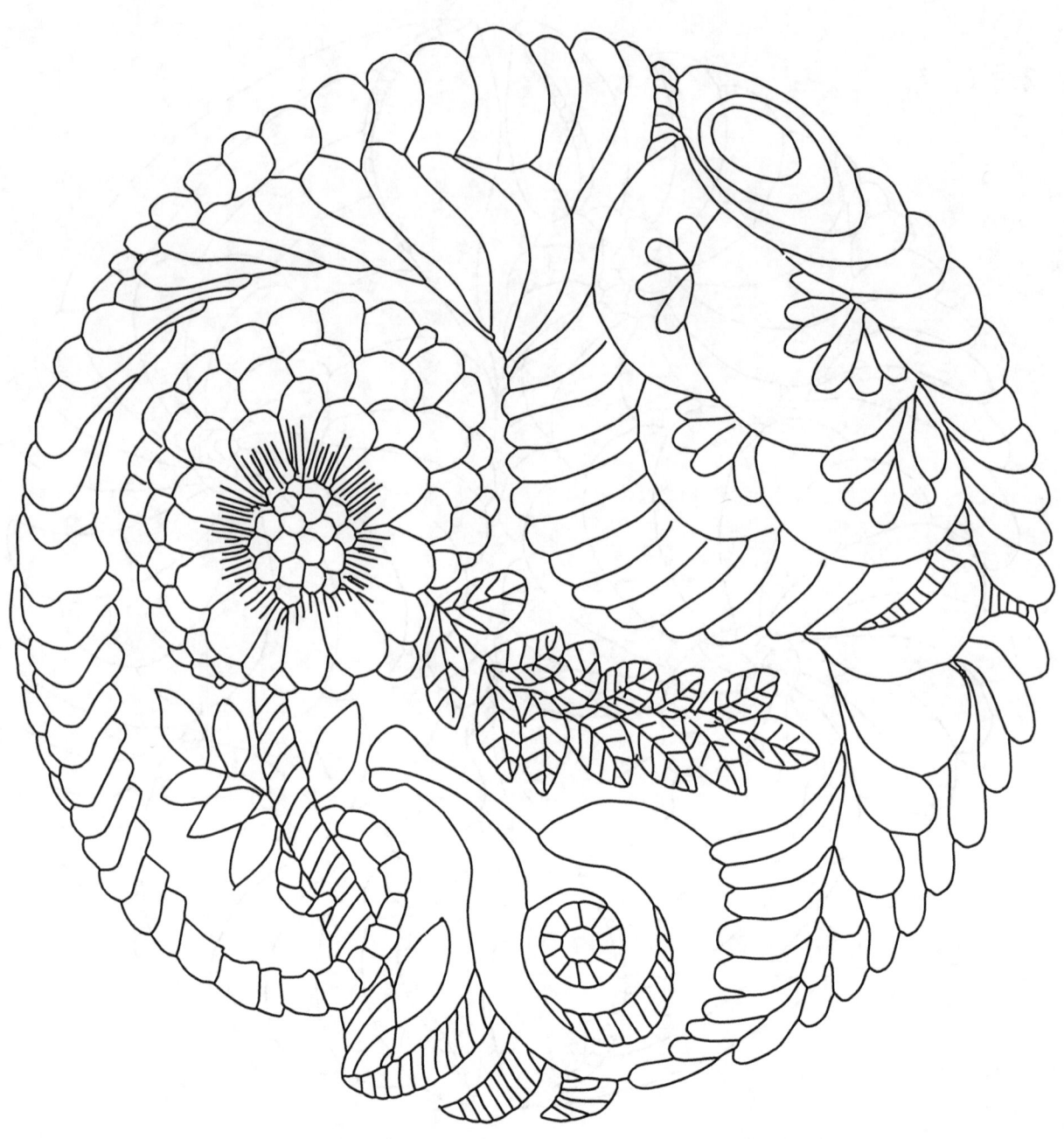

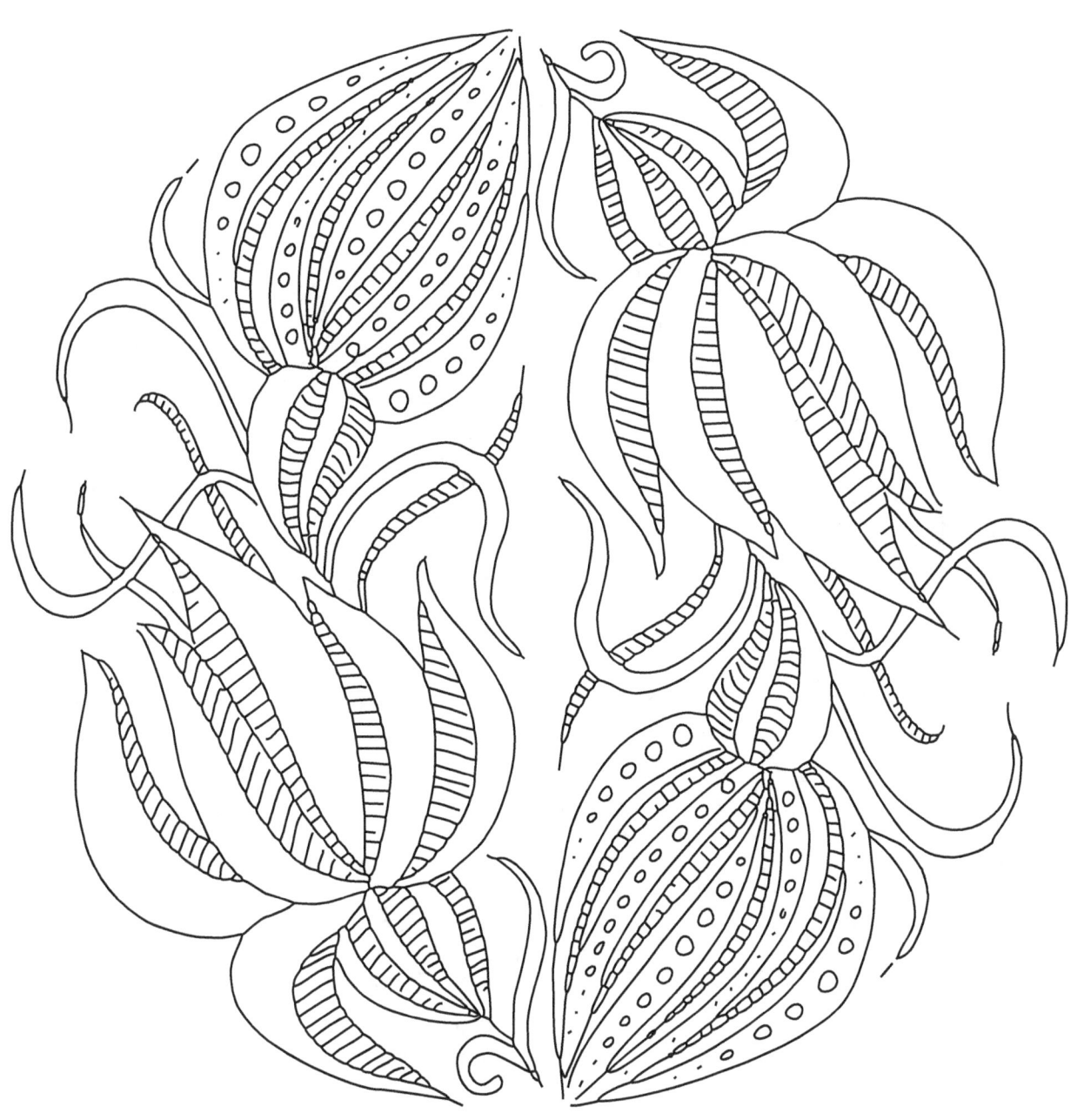

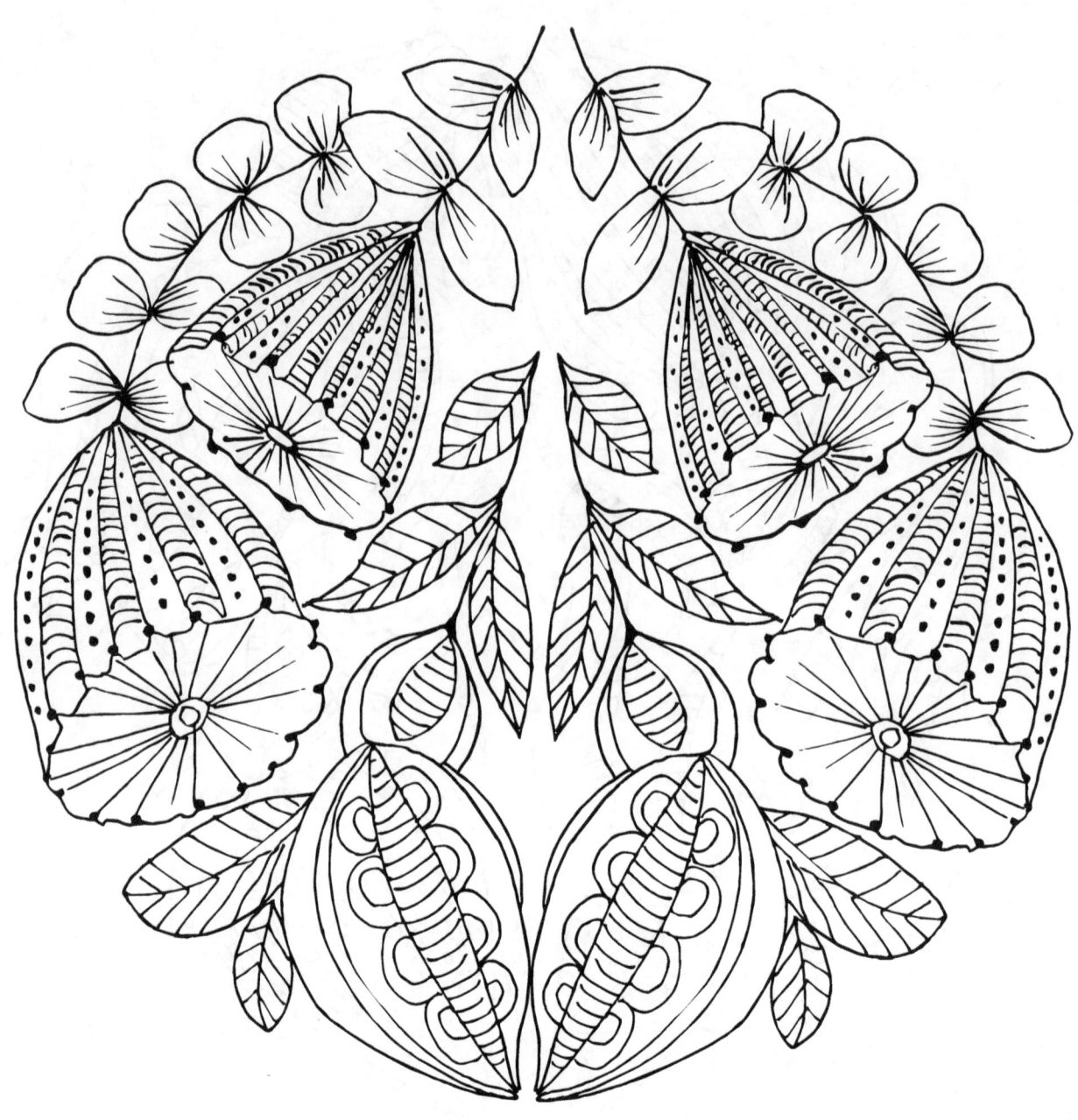

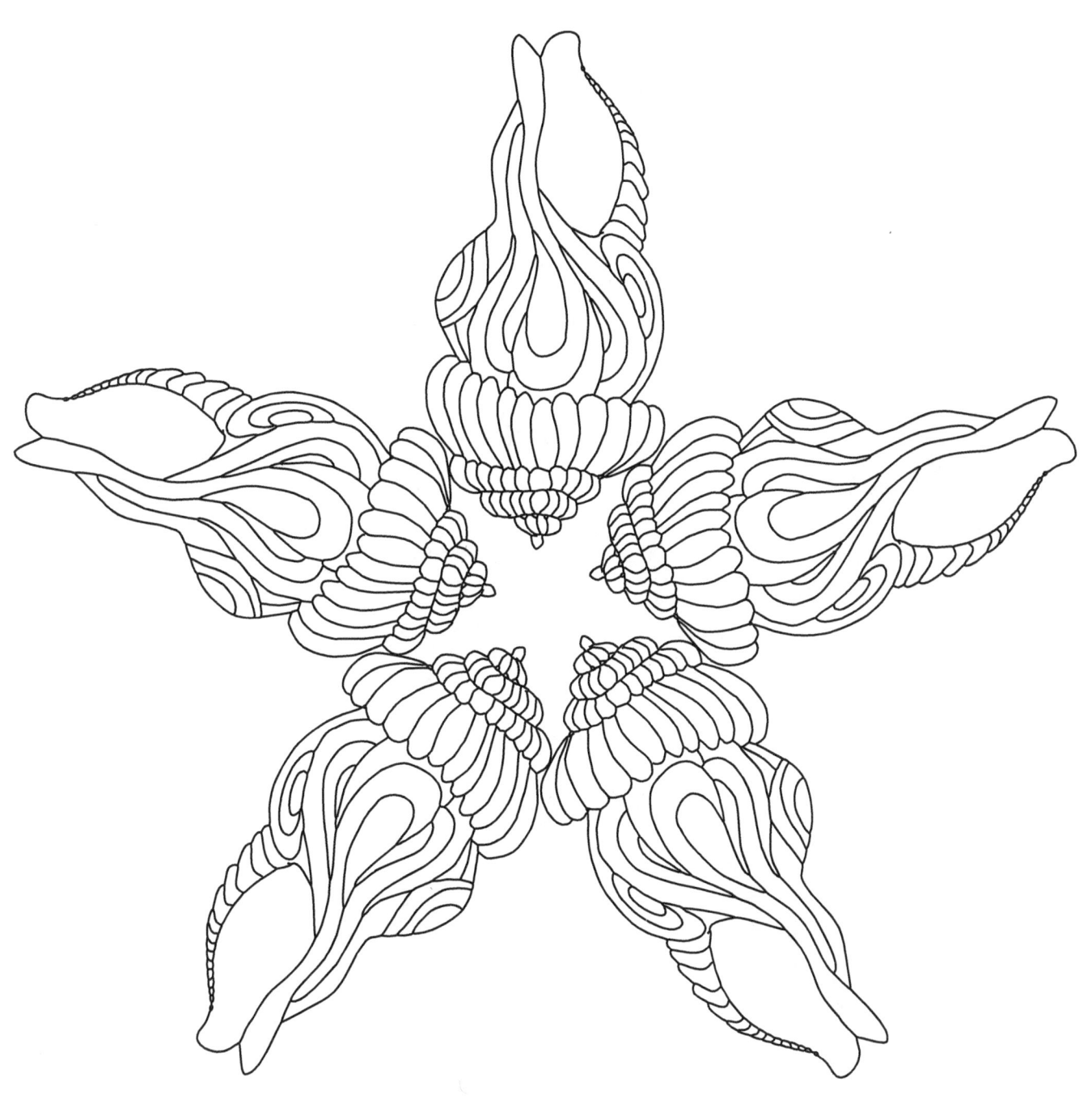

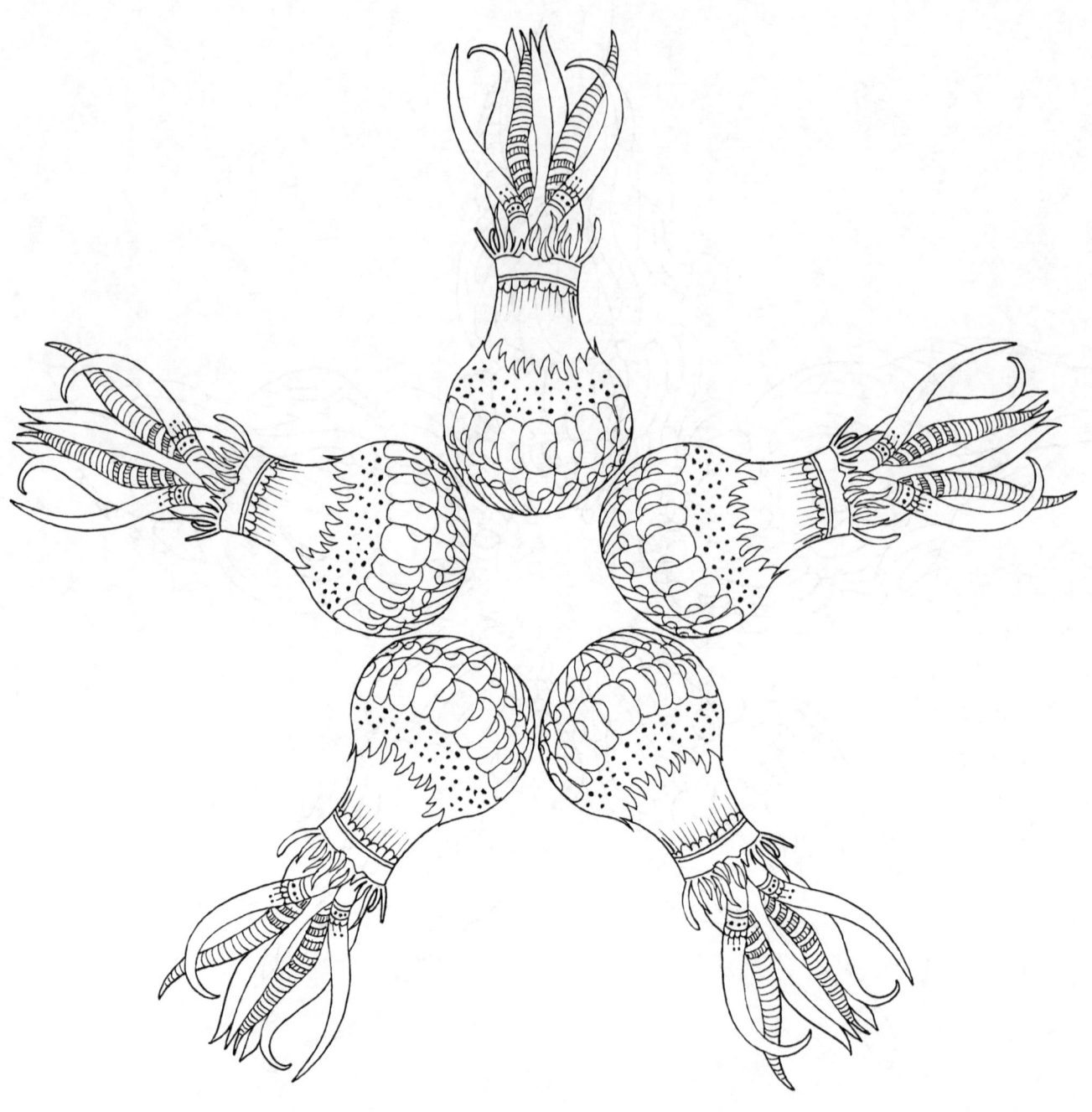

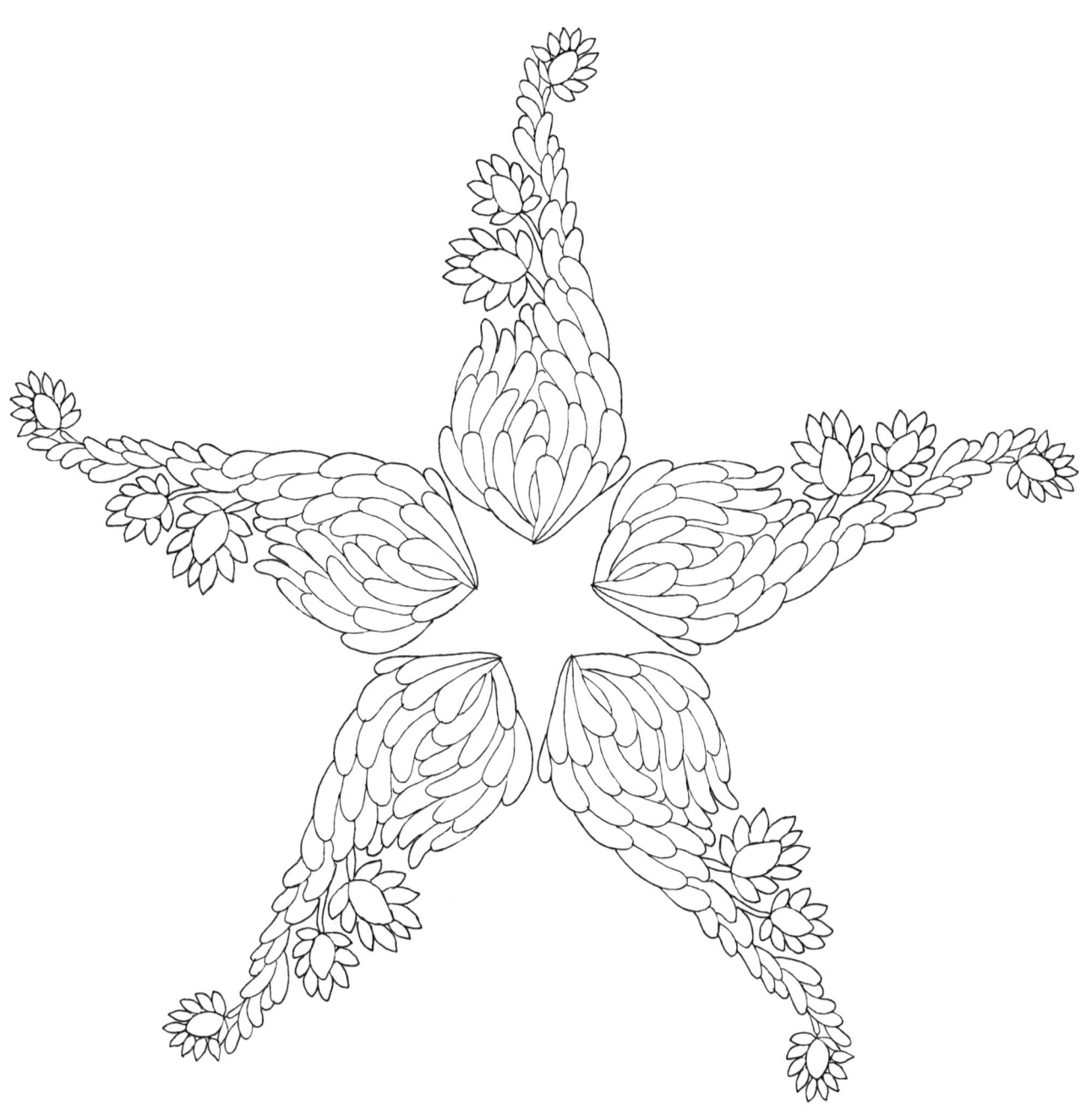

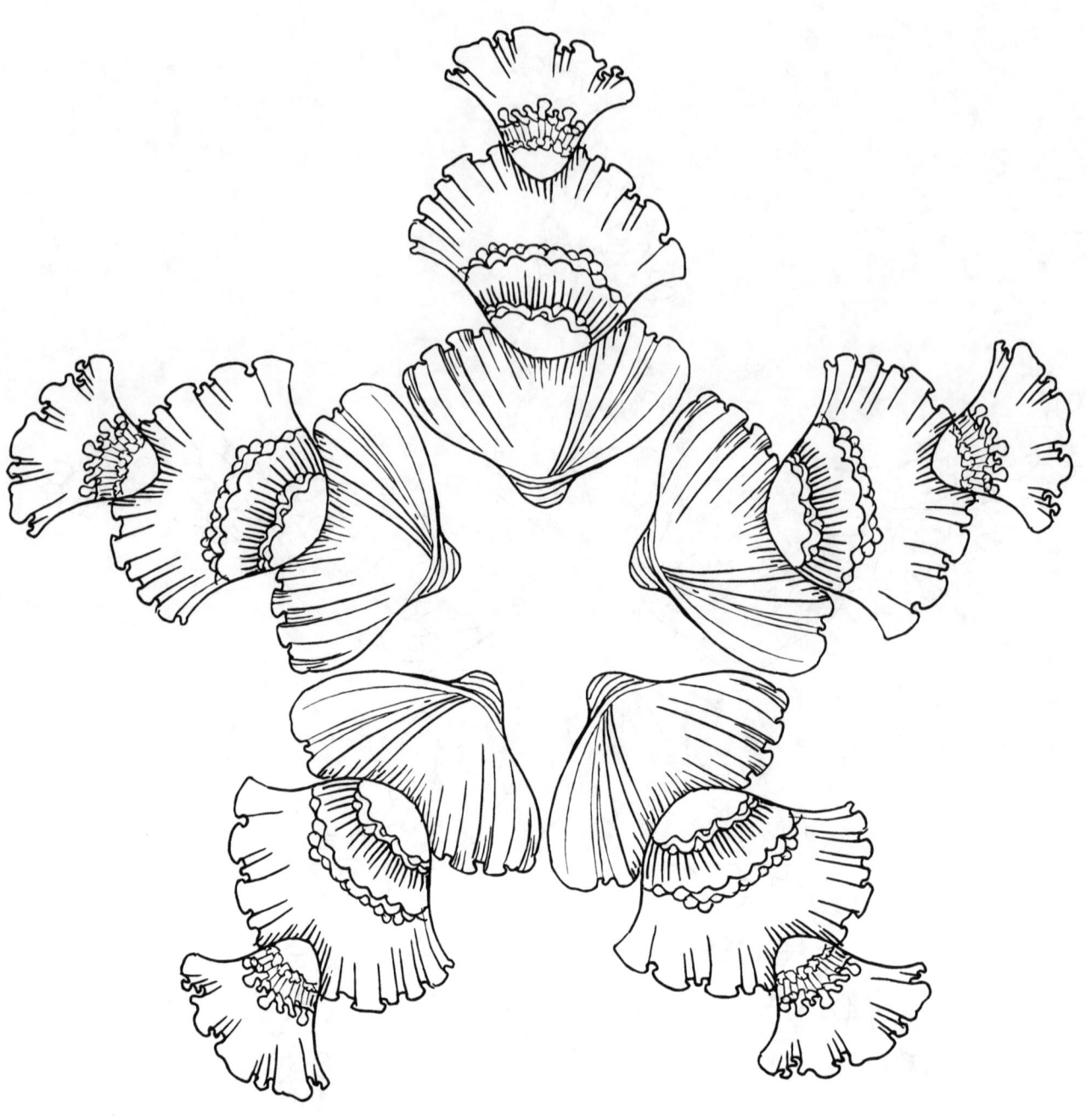

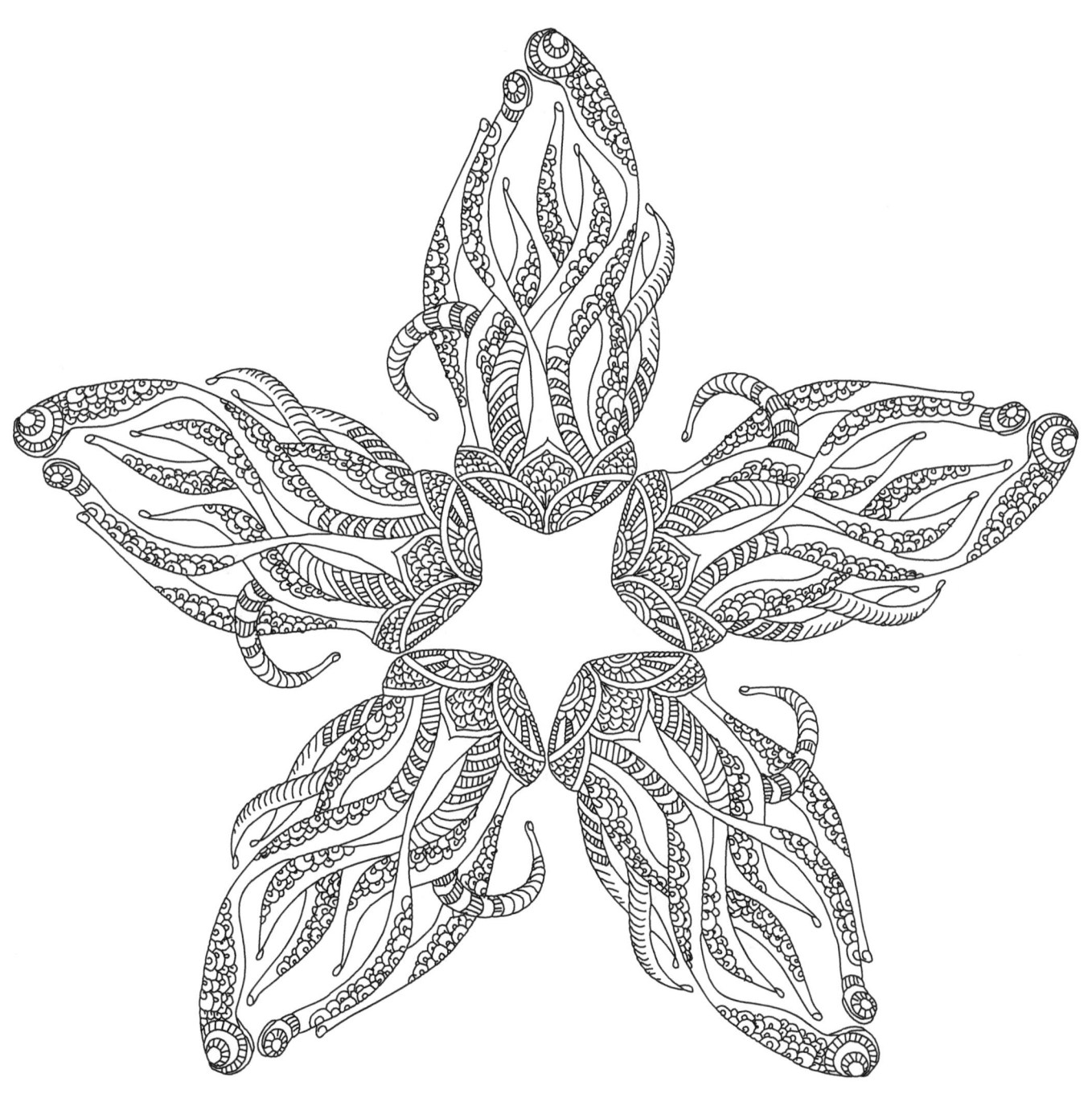

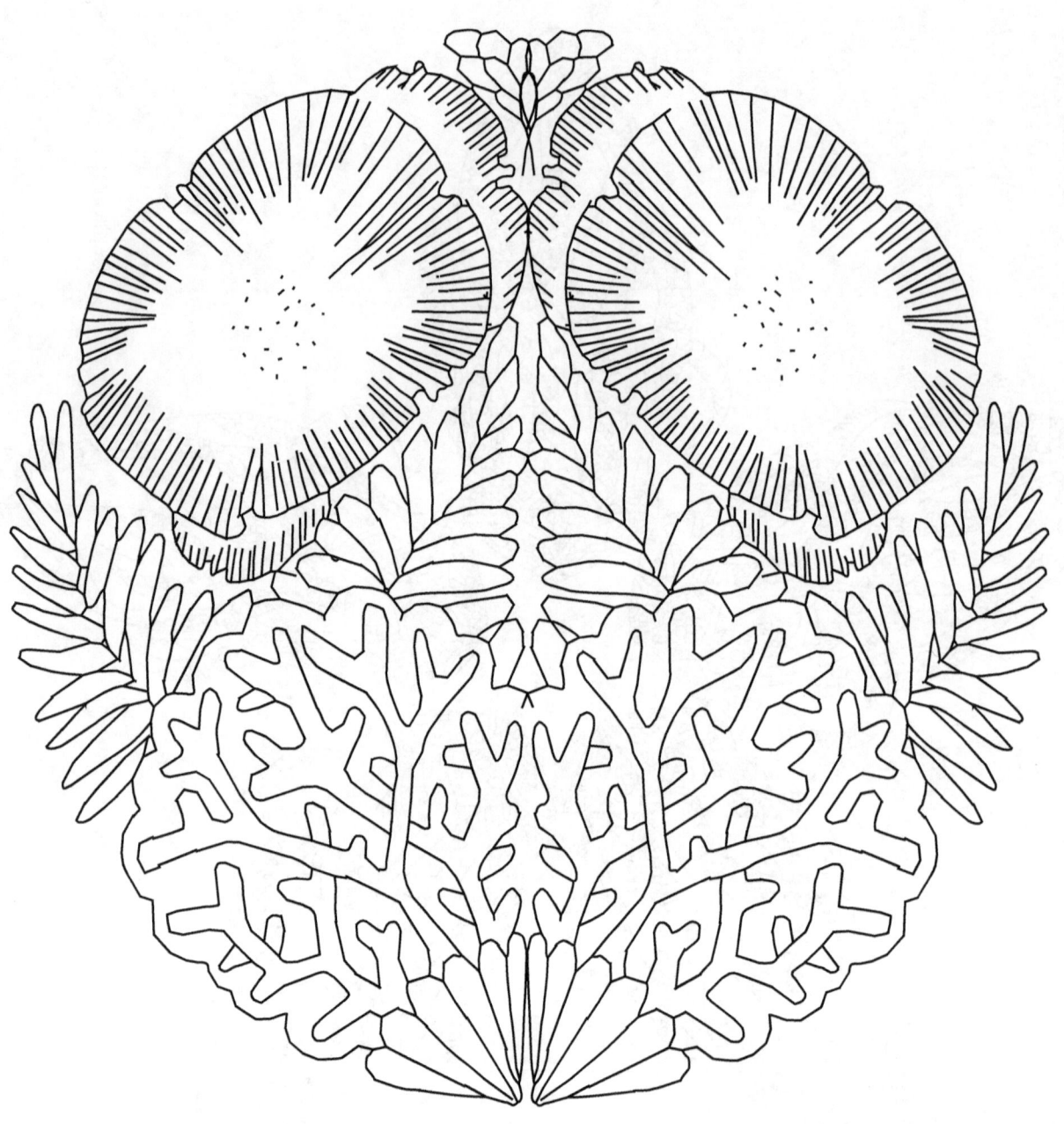

www.ingramcontent.com/pod-product-compliance
Lightning Source LLC
Chambersburg PA
CBHW080558190526
45169CB00007B/2814